Empowered COO

Eliminate Burnout, Resentment and Self Doubt as a Second-in-Command

Rachel Lebowitz

Foreword by Douglas Brackmann Ph.D.

Empowered COO

Independently Published

Copyright © 2024, Rachel Lebowitz

Published in the United States of America

230927-02389.3.1

ISBN: 9798329351194

Dedication

To my dear husband Ezra, the most fascinating, flaming visionary I have ever met.

This book is the culmination of experiencing life by your side; as the yin to your yang, you are the greatest gift I could ever ask for.

Here's What's Inside...

Praise for Empowered COO

*"Rachel's book, **Empowered COO**, shares a unique insight you haven't seen anywhere else. She came to the insights and recommendations she teaches in this book after studying addiction, being a codependency coach, being part of a fast-growing entrepreneurial business married to its founder, and learning from scores of sessions with leadership teams as a Professional EOS Implementer. This book will show you where the Visionary/Integrator dynamics come from and what strategies COOs/2ICs can use to become less enmeshed, more effective, happier, more successful, and less burned out."*

Ben Wolf, Founder and CEO of Wolf's Edge Integrators and author of Fractional Leadership

"Empowered COO is an indispensable guide to navigating the often-challenging Visionary/Integrator relationship. Tailored specifically for Integrators who feel overwhelmed by their Visionary's constant need for speed, changing priorities, and never-ending new ideas, this book offers a lifeline. It's packed with actionable tips and real-world examples. It's a must-read for any Integrator seeking to transform exhaustion into empowerment and chaos into collaboration."

Amy Holtz, classic Visionary, EOS Implementer

"Rachel has done an amazing job weaving the relationship between CEOs and COOs and the current understanding of executive structures today, the psychological and emotional dynamics that exist, and the codependence that can be so prevalent, along with tools to address each of these. And, if you find yourself in these positions, you will find this book very helpful."

Ken Richardson
Retired Therapist of 47 years, an expert in codependence and addictions. Currently working as a Personal Development Coach and Consultant.
https://kmrcaz.com

"Rachel understands the critical role of a COO. As an EOS Implementer in business and as a wife married to a Visionary and mother to multiple children. She lives an empowered life, and this book will help COOs get empowered and understand their mission and purpose, and the best ways to achieve them."

Justin Breen, EPIC F.I.T Network CEO

Foreword
by Douglas A. Brackmann Ph.D.

In the 30 years of working as a Licensed Clinical Psychologist and exclusively working in the Driven entrepreneur's world for the last 15 years, I have never found a more challenging and rewarding relationship to focus on as between the designated Driven Visionary and the often-assigned Integrator or Second-in-Command.

These "couples" come to me usually after their professional capacities have been defined, but both are at wit's end with each other. They come to me baffled and deeply struggling in their often-overlooked personal dynamics, typically filled with mistrust, deep resentment, and burnout. This is possibly the most critical relationship the company and often both parties involved can enter in their lifetime.

Rachel takes this relationship head-on and does a masterful job of capturing the complexities and struggles, as well as offering practical solutions.

Over the last five years since writing Driven, I often get the question: "Why did you write it?" The simplest truth is that I did not want to experience "being alone" as a Driven.

Over the last five years, the exponentially advancing brain scanning technology of fMRI and the vast amount of research in ADD/ADHD/Autism Spectrum strongly supports how different we are in our neurodiversity and brain function from Second-in-Commands and the rest of the world. We, Drivens, operate in a world that is not built for us. The COO is tasked to create this bridge from the abstract vision into a practical and achievable reality. Drivens clearly need them, yet these relationships are often filled with turmoil and misunderstandings.

As a result, we may feel inside like no one truly understands what it is like to be us, yet we desperately want to be understood, seen, and connected to others. When this inner psychological conflict is combined with the genetically and biologically spurred sensations of "impending doom" (specifically the DrD2-A1 and DrD4-7r genetics), there is a natural tendency for Drivens to build an identity around these emotions. This can create a sense of shame that is literally an internal hell filled with insecurities and self-loathing. This "shadow" must be hidden from the world lest we be rejected. This explains why Drivens are plagued with imposter syndrome and struggle with intimacy. Some attempt to numb this curse, falling into addictions of all kinds to escape this internal hell.

All these curses of being Driven cannot be solved in isolation. We must find a way to have trusted and collaborative relationships.

Before getting the new understanding of identity presented in Driven, our highly emotionally charged inner worlds feel most at home in a world of chaos and drama, which is why we are so at home in the early start-up environment of the entrepreneur. Genetically and neurochemically, we feel as if there is something "wrong" all the time. In nearly all new business ventures, this is true. As the company matures, grows, and has some success, without help, the Driven Visionary may unknowingly create, maintain, or even enable an outer world that seems stuck in a chaotic loop. Nowhere is the curse of chaos more evident than in our relationships with others, whether Driven or not, and yet because we are plagued with "aloneness," we are painfully aware of our need for trusted and mutually beneficial relationships.

I believe the most important aspect of this book is her addressing the psychological dynamics of the Second-in-Command. The Visionary often gets all the attention, the research, the glory, and the accolades for success, while the Integrators are often overlooked. The Integrator can be gun-shy about speaking up, which is frequently minimized by the Visionary.

The Second-in-Command can forego their own needs in the attempt to win the Visionary's approval, which plays into patterns often learned in childhood. They may shy away from any attention that can suit the Self-Focused Driven, yet as the company matures, the COO may be forced into the spotlight and grow or be left behind. The utmost importance for the

Integrator to be understood by the Visionary is something I have overlooked professionally.

Her insights into how Second-in-Commands are easily lost in the attention given to the Visionary are priceless to my practice and my clients. The Integrator's loss of self, poor boundaries, people-pleasing, and "Other-Focused" nature may have drawn the Integrator into the opportunity to work with the big personality of the Visionary.

The COO is assigned the task of creating order out of the Visionary's chaos and bringing it to life. Often, they must fight against a seemingly unwilling and defensive-driven Visionary who is shy on praise, constantly filled with an unquenchable urgency, and often makes impulsive decisions to change course quickly. What a nearly impossible task for Second-in-Commands!

Rachel captures the dynamics between this odd coupling in a way that brings it to life and offers practical exercises and pointed questions that all lead to solutions to create a highly effective relationship. Rachel does a wonderful job not only articulating the skills needed to be developed by the COO but also includes practical tools and worksheets to guide the process. Enjoy!

Introduction

If you picked up this book, you probably are an Integrator/COO or Second-in-Command. Maybe you are a Visionary entrepreneur who wants to better understand the dynamics of your Second-In-Command relationship. If you are the Visionary, I applaud and thank you for supporting your Second-In-Command.

The following experience might sound familiar: You are hired or promoted as the Integrator/COO, and everyone has high hopes and expectations that you will perform phenomenally in your role. The company's Visionary is excited and confident that they have finally found the perfect puzzle piece. They see you as the knight in shining armor who will save them from themselves; from their need for chaos, from their constant new ideas, and from their need for speed. You bring the promise of order, organization, systems, and the role of filter to all ideas, and the player who will bring the amazing ones into reality. But somewhere along the line, there is a switch. Sometimes, this shift happens six months into your role, sometimes a year, and sometimes five years. As the Integrator/COO, you find yourself resentful, exhausted, burnt out, and disconnected. There is a rapid deterioration of your confidence and an undeniable gap. You are unsure how the fissure happened or how to bridge and repair it. You start dreading your role, your self-care wanes, and you begin living by rote and realize that you have lost your spark. You become slow at making decisions, unenthusiastic about the Visionary's constant churn of ideas, and the concept of bringing them into reality feels daunting.

The COO role, by nature, is all about fulfilling someone else's vision. The best Second-In-Command (a word I will abbreviate as 2IC and use interchangeably for Integrator and COO) is anyone who is the right-hand person to a Visionary/entrepreneur/founder of an organization). In this role, you can quickly lose yourself, neglect your own needs, and become entangled in the mission of bringing the Visionary or entrepreneur's ideas into reality. This role naturally presents challenges of isolation and uncertainty. It feels like your output is 120%, and you are only being reciprocated by 50% in commitment and recognition. You live and breathe a business that is not even yours. You feel misunderstood and secretly resentful for taking on so much and have difficulty saying no. Without clearly defined functions, meaning your role is not clearly defined as it is constantly changing and evolving based on the business's needs, it is easy to get lost. Additionally, all the challenges and miscommunications with Visionaries keep causing partnership breakups. It is exhausting to battle two fronts: Bringing the Visionary's ideas into reality while leading, managing, and holding accountable the leadership team. No small wonder that you are also struggling with burnout.

How do I know all this?

I am not an Integrator.

I am a Visionary married to a Visionary (that is a lot of fun and deserves a separate book).

Over the years, I have become obsessed with analyzing people's behavior patterns. I grew up in our family business and was fascinated by how employees acted when the boss was around versus when he was not. That propelled me to study business behavioral science. Fast forward many years later, I am the spouse of a Visionary, I am a codependence recovery coach, and I am an EOS Implementer. (An EOS implementer is a business coach who helps business owners and their leadership teams implement companywide systems. This creates clarity around the business vision. We then elucidate goals and create accountability based on those goals, which ultimately leads to a healthy, open, honest, and cohesive environment where everyone wants to work and prosper.) I have spent a lot of time observing and coaching Visionaries, their spouses, spouses of people with addiction, and many COOs.

In my work, I notice patterns of challenges that arise for individuals in supportive roles, whether at home or in a company. Many diminish themselves, feel guilty when putting themselves first, become overly passive, fear being disliked or rejected, or turn to control. They become enmeshed and excessively dependent on the Visionary's approval and other people's opinions.

You might not even be aware that you subconsciously feel all these things. You may come across as strong and authoritative. You are known as the caretakers of the world. Some call you the "salt of the earth," going the extra mile and always available to jump in and fill gaps. But somehow, you find yourself lonely, resentful, and neglecting to care for yourself.

I am here to tell you it does not have to be this way. My passion is empowering supportive figures like you to find your voice, step into your power, and get back in touch with yourself so that you can become your best self—which ultimately benefits everyone.

Right now, there is a gap in self-development resources for people in supportive roles. Visionaries and entrepreneurs can access programs like Genius Network, EO, YPO, and Vistage. Yet, you and all the 2ICs have very few resources. There is the COO Forum, Rocket Fuel, and COO Alliance. These resources focus heavily on the relationship between 2ICs and Visionaries and less on helping COOs restore and focus their confidence on a healthy sense of self. They also don't have specialized support. Often, they receive advice and guidance from Visionary experts instead of experts who understand the unique challenges and psychological makeup of a person in a supportive role.

This ill-fitted matchup is also found in the world of addiction treatment. The addicts get specialized treatment from addiction specialists, and the spouses are treated by the same professional. The spouse really needs a specialist in the field of codependence.

As we all know, the COO brings the Visionary's ideas and visions to life, and without you, there is no accomplishing those big goals.

In this book, I aim to provide behavioral science and supportive resources specifically for COOs.

I aim to help you transition from self-doubt, burnout, and resentment to becoming an assertive leader. I want to equip you with the soft skills—like discernment, decisiveness, and assertiveness—that distinguish the top 2.5 percent of 2ICs.

I regularly witness 2ICs transform as they connect with their strengths and desires. Sometimes, this growth leads them to move on, as often happens when one partner evolves.

The tools in this book will empower you. You will feel energized and not depleted. You will gain a clear sense of self and not enmeshment with others. You will become respected leaders who drive results.

Rachel

PART ONE

Chapter One
What Is a 2IC?

A 2IC is the right hand of any Visionary entrepreneur. They are the highest level of authority reporting to the Visionary. The term "Second-in-Command" literally explains what this role is. First-in-Command is the organization's Visionary, founder, or entrepreneur; their right-hand person is called the Integrator, Second-in-Command, or COO, which we call 2IC.

In the business version of a marriage, a Visionary and 2IC are the spouses. If you have been married long enough, you will realize that the notion that marriages are 50/50 is wishful thinking. Marriage is about highlighting each other's positive traits and bringing out the best in each other to build something beautiful together. In a marriage, you have mutual respect for each other, value each other's opinions equally, and you don't argue in front of your kids.

Sometimes, one side gives 80%, and the other gives 20% and other times, it's the opposite. There is a constant yin and yang to balance each other.

The same applies to a healthy Visionary and 2IC relationship. For any committed relationship to be productive and successful there must be a high level of trust. You need to "get" each other. If you live with someone long enough, know each other, and are in sync, you tend to finish each other's sentences and know what will make the other person happy, angry, or tick them off. You become an extension of each other, intrinsically connected. Yet have a healthy sense of interdependence and respect.

This book is about gaining a deep understanding of the innate skills of top-performing 2ICs and the differences in personality between Visionaries and 2ICs. What makes them tick? What makes them stick? How are Visionaries and 2ICs different? How can you reconcile the differences to "get" each other, understand yourself, and understand the Visionary better? How can you bring the best version of yourself to the table? How can you be an empowering force that brings vitality and life to the organization or business?

In the book *Rocket Fuel*, Gino Wickman and Mark C. Winters define a 2IC or Integrator as; "They are the glue, the Visionary's right hand. They beat the drum and ensure trains run on time".

They define the Integrator as somebody who brings clarity, communication, resolution, focus, accountability, team unity, prioritization, follow-through, execution, and more. It is best to read Gino and Mark's book, *Rocket Fuel*, and check out www.rocketfueluniversity.com to see a detailed description of a 2IC and the defined job description and accountabilities.

The roles described are all intangible soft skills that a BA in college won't help you attain. Gino and Mark essentially say that the 2IC has excellent project management, people, and strategy skills.

In more practical terms, a 2IC is like a party planner. They walk into the room, and in their mind's eye, they can see the whole checklist of tasks that need to be done to make this party happen. They are great at connecting and listening to the concerns of all people involved, from the host to the caterer to the waiters, making sure everyone feels heard and understands their role in pulling off this amazing wedding.

The 2IC runs the day-to-day coordination and operation of an organization. They ensure all functions, like sales, marketing, operations, and finance, work together. They are the ones that take the Visionary's ideas from up in the clouds and bring them down into reality. They are great at executing plans, mapping out projects, following through on ideas, and filtering the Visionary's dreams so everyone stays on track to achieve the greater good and goal of the company.

In his book, *The Second-in-Command, Unleash the Power of Your COO*, Cameron Harold describes the CEO and Second-in-Command relationship as a homeowner and a general contractor. Let's say you are building a house, and you hire a contractor. Does your contractor decide the style and color of the walls, or does the homeowner? Let's say you want an obscenely huge three-story high dining room. Your contractor will say, "Well, that can be done, but it will cost you $200,000 of steel. Your house will always be cold because there is so much open space. How will you change a light bulb on such a high ceiling?" That is the voice of the 2IC exercising discernment. It is not coming up with a concept but instead bringing it into reality, laying out the pieces, weighing the benefits and drawbacks, and ultimately facilitating a decision.

I will not delve into the responsibilities and accountabilities of the 2IC. I will preface this book by saying it is imperative to learn the foundation first. A great place to start is Rocket Fuel Academy. It is free and chock full of resources to help you – as the 2IC, get clarity on your roles and responsibilities.

Read the above-mentioned books and utilize the essential resources, especially if you are new to this role.

Different Types of 2ICs

What is the role of a 2IC? How does it play out in real-life? First, it is essential to understand the different types of 2ICs. A great way to understand this concept is the Integrator continuum by keystone search: https://keystonesearch.com/Integrator-continuum/

KEYSTONE INTEGRATOR CONTINUUM™

People Mgmt Process Mgmt Metrics Mgmt	Coach/Mentor Develop skills	Right Structure Right Seats Cohesion	Strategy Development Market Trends Product Relevance Service Offerings	Thought Partner Collaboration on Vision "Prozac"
Manage PPM	People Development	Organizational Development	Business Planning	Advisor
SMALLER PROJECTS		LARGER PROJECTS		
	Functional Projects Shorter Time Frames		Enterprise Wide Mission Critical Longer/Complex	

In smaller businesses, from solopreneurs to 10-15 employees, a 2IC will act more like an administrative assistant, executive assistant, general manager, or office manager. This is presented on the left side of the Keystone Integrator Continuum^{TM}. The 2IC on this end of the spectrum makes sure that things are running on time and that tasks are being completed.

As a business grows and gets more complex, it involves more people and more moving parts.

The 2ICs role becomes more about managing people, processes, and metrics to ensure healthy business progress. At the same time, they continue to oversee a lot of the day-to-day business functions.

As a business grows even more, the 2IC plays a higher-level role. They become more of special project persons. They act more like a strategic partner and consultant and must be more agile, more on their toes, and more creative in figuring out complex and extensive strategies. This is represented on the right side of the Keystone Integrator Continuum^{TM}.

In a healthy Visionary/2IC relationship, there is a high level of trust, and the 2IC makes companywide, leadership team, and day-to-day decisions that pertain to cross-department matters. This is not to be confused (and is often confused) with ownership and big Visionary decisions like buying a new asset, expanding a product line, or bringing in investors.

You can think of the level 2IC that you are by using the scale of dollar amount decisions. 2ICs of small companies have the autonomy to make decisions on smaller dollar amounts than higher-level 2ICs. In a small company with $2-3 million in revenue and ten employees, the Visionary might feel comfortable giving up control over decisions that cost anywhere from $1-$5000 but would want to make any decisions that cost more than that. For higher levels of 2ICs, the responsibility and autonomy of dollar decisions are higher.

The concepts clarified in this book will appeal most to 2ICs of small to midsize companies with 10-250 employees. The ones tasked with the day-to-day business. The 2ICs that turn the Visionary's ideas into reality, ensure that things are running on-time, eliminate chaos, and are the voice of reason within the company. However, many strategic business planning 2ICs at the higher level of the spectrum will find much value and information in this book, too.

Many people believe that the difference between a 2IC at the lowest level of the spectrum and at the highest level is the hard skills you either have or don't have. Some of these skills come with experience, and some can be learned, like reading a P&L report and balance sheets.

However, personal observations and scientific studies show that soft skills are the difference between 2ICs on the lower level of the spectrum and 2ICs on the higher level of the spectrum. These are the skills that are expanded upon in this book. Essentially, it is about learning how to be assertive with leadership team members and the Visionary. It is the ability to be decisive and transparent with your expectations, needs, wants, and goals and have a healthy sense of self and boundaries. It is the ability to be a great discerner and hone in on your sense of intuition, prioritization, and strategizing to guide you and help you filter the Visionary's barrage of ideas.

Far too often, 2ICs fail to grow along with the company's needs and transition upwards on the spectrum. I believe there are so many short-term engagements of 2ICs because they are missing these crucial soft skills. The concepts in this book will help 2ICs level up so they can grow along with the needs of a growing company.

Questions to Think About:

Do you have a clear description of your role as a 2IC?

Where do you see yourself on the Keystone Integrator Continuum^{TM}?

How does it help you clarify your role?

Are there mismatched expectations between you and your Visionary on what your role should be?

What are the most challenging parts of your role?

Chapter Two
The Unspoken Challenges of 2ICs

Visionaries and entrepreneurs are typically prominent personalities. They take up a lot of space. The world is very much into promoting entrepreneurship and Visionaries. Many self-development groups exist for CEOs, such as Strategic Coach, Vistage, Genius Network, and EO, to name a few! There are fewer resources for 2ICs. I can list less than a handful: The Integrator Mastery Forum, COO Alliance, and The COO Forum. COOs are often forgotten.

What are the challenges of the 2IC? What is it like to be that Second-In-Command, the person in the supportive role?

There are many "unspoken" challenges. It is simply not spoken about. We need to address the psychology, the way 2ICs operate, and what makes them so great and valuable. We must ask, "What do you need in order to be your best? What are your goals and aspirations for your role and future? Are you at your best?

How can we help you so you can assist the Visionary with bringing to life their vision?"

In the book *Rocket Fuel*, Gino Wickman and Mark C. Winters discuss what the job of a 2IC should look like, the tools needed, and a lot about the "relationship" per se. Still, there is no dedicated handy guide for the 2IC who find themselves in a bind, in that gap, where you wake up and realize you feel used up and alone, and you don't know why.

Why is There No Clarity Around the 2IC Role?

The traditional setup of organizations usually includes sales, marketing, operations, finance, and human resources. Then, there is a CEO or Visionary. With his brilliance, Gino Wickman came up with the idea of an Integrator or 2IC role. Many other thought leaders have adopted this concept. Cameron Herald calls it a COO or Second-in-Command, whereas traditionally, a COO would be a Chief Operating Officer. Some people confuse that with the Head-of-Operations. Yet, the Head-of-Operations is solely accountable for the company's operations. As a Head-of- Operations, once the sale is made, the question becomes what do I need to do to ensure that everything in my jurisdiction gets executed to get my product or service out to my customer?

A COO, on the other hand, takes care of all the departments. However, there needs to be clarity around it because, for every organization, the 2IC or COO role means something different. Every organization has different roles and what is needed to fill that seat. That is what the Keystone Integrator Continuum^{TM} tries to clarify.

A startup needs the 2IC to do a lot of marketing research and to hire the right marketing team. When a company is more established, the 2IC needs to figure out how to create systems and processes that save money, produce a product, and sell it efficiently.

Another invisible challenge is that Visionaries are scared to let go of the vine and allow the 2ICs to take charge of day-to-day company decisions. This is because Visionaries do not have clarity around the difference between ownership, Visionary, and Second-in-Command types of decisions. For example, buying an investment is an ownership decision. Establishing revenue goals or the culture of the company is a Visionary decision. Deciding which system to use for quality control is a Second-in-Command decision.

The 2IC is best poised and primarily responsible for making decisions, both big and small, that will improve the day-to-day operations.

Because there are so many different types of Visionaries, there are many types of 2ICs. Therefore, when defining the seat, no universal description fits exactly. This creates complications and is the cause for misunderstandings and the lack of clarity.

Unintentional 2ICs

As an EOS Implementer, one of the first steps in creating clarity and accountability in organizations is sitting in a room with the organization's leadership team and creating an accountability chart. This is an organizational chart on steroids. We always want to understand "who's who in the zoo." We are giving names and roles to seats to ensure people know what they are accountable for so they can execute.

When we get to the 2IC seat, we say, "okay. WHO wants this role?" from my experience, I often find that the person who volunteers has high follow-through, is excellent at executing, and usually is someone who likes to please others and may have a hard time saying no. There is a magnetic attraction between the types of people who tend to fall into this seat and Visionaries. Unknowingly, they fall into a role that entails being the middleman. Managing two fronts: the leadership team and the Visionary's ideas.

Imagine the Visionary's big personality and the Visionary's tendency to create chaos within an organization. Visionaries tend to do that; they come up with many ideas, walk in, and say, "Oh, my gosh. I have this great idea". Suddenly, everybody gets excited because that is the Visionary's strength. Visionaries can get you excited about the most random things. Then, everybody wants to rally around that.

But sometimes, it is a distraction and not for the company's greater good. The 2IC must be excellent at filtering these ideas. If you do not have an assertive 2IC that says, "Wait. Let's look at this. Maybe it is a great idea, but should we do it now or later?" you are setting the organization up for chaos, failure and stunted growth.

If the person in the seat of the 2IC is only a yes person, then we are only solving half the problem and creating many other systemic issues like an underdeveloped team that doesn't make independent decisions. In such a case, the Visionary becomes a genius with many helping hands like an octopus but can never indeed rise above the organization to go out and expand the vision of the company. The 2IC is only performing half of their duties by saying yes to every idea instead of also developing the assertive skills to filter and implement ideas at the right time.

The 2IC Role is Lonely

2ICs are isolated because there is no peer at that level. You have the Visionary on top of you and the leadership team under you. But it would be best if you had someone parallel to you who has an understanding of the challenges that you are going through. It would be inappropriate for a 2IC to go to the Head-of-Sales and say, "I am having such a hard time getting the Visionary to come around and understand why expanding our business right now is a bad idea or investing in a different vertical is a bad idea." That is like one parent venting and badmouthing another parent to the kids. We all know how dysfunctional that is. It often becomes very lonely because they are pushing back on two fronts and do not have anybody parallel to them on their level.

2ICs are also very much occupied with the inside of the business and tend not to socialize as much as Visionaries and CEOs. They don't usually go to conferences, masterminds, and networking events where they would have the opportunity to meet other 2ICs, share opportunities and challenges, get feedback, and have companion relationships.

Living in the Gap

A gap gradually develops between Visionaries and 2ICs if not proactively addressed. There is a lot of talk about "a company is only as healthy as the Visionary," leadership and culture come from the top, etc. The world has realized how significant personal growth and emotional intelligence are to the success and health of companies. That is why CEOs are strongly encouraged to become healthier and invest in their personal development. By now, there is a whole industry built around it. Seminars, summits, Tony Robins, and being part of groups like Vistage, EO, Strategic Coach, and Genius Network. 2ICs have very little such exposure or access. They work in the day-to-day business but are not gaining knowledge about business development and, most importantly, personal growth and emotional intelligence.

What I have personally seen happen in many companies is that Visionaries are growing, but 2ICs are not. Visionaries are growing fast and are fast adapters. They love growth. They love change. 2ICs stay in the day-to-day, and they don't like change. They are doing what they know best, but without developing and updating their skills and staying "in the know," a gap widens.

The Visionary grows, and the 2ICs stay where they are. One day, the Visionary wakes up and says, "I do not love this relationship anymore. We are not on the same page." Because the Visionary has been introduced to more tools, skills, and methodologies than the 2IC, they are no longer in sync; they are not constantly catching up with each other and growing together as a team.

It is like when a couple falls out of "love." One spouse went and did their work, went to therapy, grew, changed, and the other spouse stayed left behind. Now, there is a gap that is sometimes irreparable.

What Is in It for Them?

A pivotal moment for my support around 2ICs was at the 2023 EOS Conference in Indianapolis. Mark C. Winters, the co-author of *Rocket Fuel*, was discussing the importance of the CEO-COO relationship.

He was delving into the stamina and tenacity needed to be a great Visionary and build a fantastic leadership team. Toward the end of his presentation, he showed a slide with a big mountain and the Visionary on top of the hill.

The title said, "All is well because my Integrator's got this." This means that the Visionary won his pursuit of freedom; they are out in the world, with the freedom to climb mountains, expand their horizons, and they credit the 2IC for holding it all together. After all, the 2ICs hold down the company's day-to-day operations and ensure that everything runs on time, like a Swiss watch.

At that moment, I felt a pain in my stomach. I was thinking, "What is in it for them? What is in it for those Integrators? What in the big picture are we selling for 2ICs?" In most cases, COOs are not stakeholders or partners. Yet, they dedicate their whole life to this business, day in and day out. At the end of the day, what is in it for them? Visionaries have the advantage of "making money while they sleep," setting up a self-managed business with the help of a 2IC and team so they can utilize their unique ability and do anything they can dream of. Visionaries exist on big dreams. "When I have X million in the bank, I will buy myself that nice house, a fancy car, and a big vacation." 2ICs, on the other hand, have less tolerance for risk and want stability and security. Yet, are we giving them a promise or pledge of security for dedicating their hearts and souls to a business that isn't theirs?

It signified the importance of doing better for our 2ICs and COOs. We need to give them a personal long-term vision and sense of security.

I have spoken to many 2ICs who feel stiffed because they have helped companies grow from millions to billions, only to be sold and left with no payout or job.

One 2IC, let's call him Jonathan, shares how he quickly grew his Visionary's company from 3 million to 300 million over four years. Jonathan was pretty assertive in the way he dealt with his Visionary. He moved growth along, prevented chaos, and was successful in transitioning up the Integrator Continuum from general manager to strategic thinker. Yet, he feels resentful for having the rug pulled from under his feet when, after three years, the owners decided to sell the company. Not only did he not get any compensation when they sold, but it also left him job hunting all over again. Jonathan says that he wished he had a support system that would have coached him in asking for his needs and communicating his expectations for compensation for investing all his hard work into growing the company.

Every COO, at one point or another, has a fleeting moment of fear of outgrowing their seat. If a 2IC does their job well, they should be working themselves out of a job. The business will evolve, requiring a new type of 2IC on the continuum, and often, if the current 2IC doesn't adapt and grow fast enough, they are no longer the right fit for the new demands of the role. Visionaries have to remember that if they want the COO to do great work, there is even greater importance in giving them assurance and security of their future and their ideal vision for them within the company and in their personal life.

My Concern for the COO

On a global level, my concern is that we don't have enough Empowered COOs walking the planet. Gino Wickman and Mark C. Winters in *Rocket Fuel* discuss this and say, "Finding Integrators in small businesses ($2-50 million) is hard. One recruiter noted, "There's a gap in the world." According to one profiling expert, "Only about 22% of the world is even cut out to become a Visionary", yet the real problem pops up when he explains that only 5.5% of the world is truly cut out to be an Integrator. That leaves us with a daunting 4:1 ratio of Visionaries to Integrators" he goes on further to say that only 10% of Integrators are a suitable match to a given Visionary resulting in only a 2.5% chance of having a proper fit between Visionary and 2IC.

As you can see, we are starting at a deficit. I believe that the massive deficit in capable COOs is not a lack of hard skills, but a simple lack of crucial soft skills that I mentioned before can be taught— assertiveness, decisiveness, and discernment. If we can train more people to have those skills, we will raise that ratio and have better, well-run businesses.

There will always be a need for great COOs as entrepreneurs are growing businesses. Driven entrepreneurs keep our economy and planet going and innovative. We need Elon Musk in all his craziness to get us to Mars and driverless cars. We need to help the world create better-run companies for the greater good of humanity and the world.

On a micro level, I am concerned about not discussing these challenges. If we do not address them and help COOs, even the best 2ICs will become worn out, burnt out, and resentful. When an entrepreneur fails, you rarely hear them say, "I am giving up on being an entrepreneur; I am going to work for someone else." That seldom happens. A true entrepreneur is unemployable, and their drive for freedom, for not being told what to do but instead going and creating something new, overrides the pain of failure.

On the other hand, in speaking to many COOs in the process of writing this book, I have come across way too many 2ICs that share a different story. They never want to work for another Visionary again. They are worn out, used up, and burnt out. They are ready to abandon their true self with the unique ability to be detail-oriented, following through on projects, filtering ideas, and bringing them into reality because they are so burnt out and fed up.

When 2ICs are in burnout and continue to run a company, then the culture deteriorates. There is complacency, a lack of accountability, delayed decision-making and slow adaptation to industry change. There are a lot of premature disengagements between CEOs and COOs. Perhaps those relationships should not be long-term, but they are much shorter than they should be. We lack insight, tools, and support for 2ICs and COOs. We can look at it the same way that we are looking at the divorce rate in the world. Divorce rates are going up because people are not doing what it takes to learn how to communicate effectively in relationships and how to honor each other's DNA. Spouses are different. You must honor each other's personality and learn to integrate and work together. When we are not doing that, we see resentment, anger, loneliness, misunderstandings, and breakups.

Questions to Think About:

Can you see a growth path for your role? Do you think you have the skills to get there?

How do you cope with loneliness in your role? Who do you confide with?

Did you unintentionally become the 2IC? Do you have what it takes to push back on both fronts?

Do you make sure to constantly learn more personally and professionally?

Do you dedicate time to sharpen your leadership skills and stay current with what your Visionary is learning in his peer groups?

Do you find yourself worrying about your future? How do you manage it?

Chapter Three
Why Do 2ICs Fall Short?

It is easy to blame all the issues I described earlier on Visionaries. After all, Visionaries are known as compulsive and driven; most have markers of attention deficit disorder, and they constantly want more and bigger and better. Yet, if we want to get to the root cause of solving all the challenges in the Visionary/2IC relationship, we must take a huge step back and acknowledge the dance that is going on here. It takes two to tango in any relationship, and the V/2IC relationship is the ultimate business marriage. So, bear with me if I am going to come across as very straightforward here. As a COO, I know that you crave empathy and compassion, yet to have a breakthrough of awareness of the dynamics at play, it is necessary for me to be very factual and straightforward.

Let's discuss what happens somewhere down the line in the Visionary/2IC or CEO/COO relationship. As the 2IC, you feel a tremendous responsibility to be the voice of reason and organization within the chaos. Often, there is mounting frustration in trying to get the Visionary to come around and see things from your perspective and understand that their ideas and timelines are not realistic or reasonable. You spend a lot of time pushing back, feeling like you have to say "NO" too often. It exhausts you.

In Walter Isaacson's book on Elon Musk, he shared countless times how Elon insisted on pushing back deadlines on space launches at SpaceX. In the beginning, his COO, Gwynne Shotwell, exerted a lot of energy trying to reason with Elon in an attempt to advocate for her people and explain why it wasn't beneficial or possible. Yet, after a while, she realized this pattern where the imposed unrealistic deadline would never happen, but Elon insisted it was still a good move because it gave him a thrill, and he sincerely believed if he didn't put everyone into hustle culture, nothing would get done. Once she had insight into what was driving Elon, she was able to be an effective 2IC by managing his shenanigans and protecting the team from Elon's wrath. In that desperate attempt to be the perfect puzzle piece and to constantly save the day, it is easy for even the best 2ICs to experience a rapid deterioration of confidence that causes them to underperform. You start losing sight of priorities and what is genuinely needed from you. Because you pay attention to detail but lose yourself under stress, you might find yourself hyper-focusing on minutia and details over the greater vision of the organization. You are worn out and exhausted from pushing back, so you slip into pleasing the Visionaries' whims rather than serving the organization's greater good. You find yourself constantly prioritizing others' needs and neglecting your own needs, thinking, "I'll get to my coffee later, I'll take off another day, it can wait," causing burnout and resentment. At the same time, you desperately want to ensure that projects are followed through, so you might resort to cajoling and over-convincing people to do things your way because you believe it is the right way and will get the job done.

You become afraid to speak-up and start avoiding conflict. You might be thinking, "It's the Visionary's business at the end of the day, so we need to make them happy and do it their way. I am just getting paid here." That inevitably puts the Visionary on a pedestal. This sense of despair and loss of confidence causes you to lose sight of your strengths and fail to maximize the value of your role. You start becoming hesitant to hold people accountable. You just want to keep the peace. You start becoming a basket case, holding it all in and finding yourself bursting from time to time.

Suzie came to me for help. The Visionary that she works for agreed to pay for the coaching as a last attempt to make her role as 2IC work. Suzie was broken and doubtful. She thought that perhaps she wasn't suited for this role after all. She shared with me how she totally lost her sense of self. In the past year, she put on a lot of weight, stopped going to the gym, and stopped socializing with friends. Even her husband was complaining that she was preoccupied and overconsumed with work and neglected her marriage and kids.

In an attempt to please the Visionary, feel useful, and gain recognition by being an indispensable employee, she has lost herself, her confidence, and her priorities. For Suzie, it was a long road to recovery. She has fallen into the codependence trap, and the gap has become too big. While she was busy focusing and being overwhelmed by things that weren't crucial for her role, like the design and layout of the company brochure and marketing materials, the company has evolved and needed a higher-level COO who can strategize and execute the next evolution of the business. Ultimately, Suzie chose to resign and stay home to focus on herself, her family, and her little kids before re-entering the workforce.

What others write off as "Oh, this person is just not fit for this role," I see the root cause of those behaviors as a loss of self-confidence caused by desperately wanting to keep the Visionary in line and control outcomes. You feel like there is this huge weight and responsibility on your shoulders to make sure the business keeps running and things get executed, and you feel overly responsible for preventing the Visionary from making poor decisions and moves. But when things get too desperate, you feel like you have lost control. Therefore, you desperately try to regain control and confidence and might hyper-focus on the unimportant details, over-please, overstretch, overdo, and act passively or aggressively, all with the drive of wanting to excel as the person that follows through, which is essential to the company's success and holds all parts of the business together including the Visionary.

This severe enmeshment and feeling that without you, the world will fall apart is called codependence. There are many aspects of codependence, but here are some that apply to the Visionary/2IC relationship.

Codependence is an emotional attachment condition where one person enables another person's compulsive behavior, immaturity, and irresponsibility or underachievement in order to validate the codependent's own need to be needed.

Dr. Ken and Mary Richardson are the founders of CODA- Codependents Anonymous, a 12-step program for recovering codependents. I have personally worked with Dr. Ken, and he says in his and Mary's professional careers, they have established that "codependence is learned patterns of unhealthy and dysfunctional thoughts, beliefs, and behaviors which adversely affect an individual's relationship with themselves and others." he goes on to say,

"Codependent thoughts and beliefs generally manifest in moderate and extreme passive and or aggressive behaviors which may include avoidant, enmeshing, and or controlling behaviors."

The results of this pattern of behaviors vary. Some people, when caught in a codependent relationship, become timid. They shrink in their seat, do not speak up, or become the opposite, over-controlling and dominant to the point where you can confuse who the Visionary and 2IC are in the relationship.

Author of *Set Boundaries, Find Peace*, Nedra Glover Tawwab, says codependence is:

- Overextending yourself (and being resentful)

- Avoiding discussions about real issues

- Cleaning up other people's messes

- Making excuses for the poor behavior of others

- Tending to others' needs and neglecting your own

- Doing things for people instead of helping them do things for themselves

- Describing other people's problems as if it is your own

- Having difficulty existing in relationships without becoming the "rescuer"

- Troubleshooting problems for others before thinking of your own

- Fixing other people's problems even when they don't ask for help

- Creating an environment where people over-rely on you, the 2IC

The crazy thing is that it's like an inevitable setup. I have seen it happen time and time again. That is because the nature of the Visionary/2IC relationship is the perfect recipe for codependence to develop and thrive. Having one person (the Visionary) be hyper-focused on goals, freedoms, and winning, while the other person's identity becomes all about feeling responsible for fixing, solving, and saving and being needed. This concept is called "Relationship Math," and I will discuss it in detail in chapter four.

The solution to this is strengthening your assertiveness, decisiveness, and discernment skills. This will give you better project management, people, and strategy skills that are necessary for a top-performing second in command. It will help you explain why you were nominated for this in the first place and elucidate your personal purpose. Not having those essential skills causes 2ICs to lose their sense of who they are and their strengths. They become just another employee following directions instead of taking initiative.

Questions to Think About:

Have you experienced a loss of confidence in your role?

Are you afraid to be assertive with the Visionary and leadership team?

Are you prioritizing helping others with their responsibilities over your own in an attempt to please and look nice?

Was there a time when you neglected your self-care in an attempt to please and take care of others first?

Chapter Four
Understanding Relationship Math

The Visionary and 2IC relationship is an "inverse attraction" relationship. This means two equal opposites cancel each other out or complete a whole. We see this often in personal relationships where two totally opposite types of people form a relationship, like a messy and tidy person or a generous and stingy person. Although they are deeply annoyed about each other's differences, they still stay together.

Yet, at the same time, an individual attracts relationships with others who are at the same level of energy, emotional intelligence, and health. It's like karma: what you put out is what you receive. How healthy you are will define the health of your relationship.

This is because there is an invisible magnetic pull at play in those relationships called "The Human Magnet Syndrome," a term coined by psychologist Ross Rosenberg. The extreme magnetic pull in such relationships goes beyond logic; it is rooted in psychology and behavioral science. This is true for the Visionary/2IC relationship, too.

Gino Wickman and Mark C. Winters call it "the perfect puzzle piece" and "Rocket Fuel" like lightning grease. But what is it that makes those relationships so electric and magnetic?

To help you understand the behavioral science behind the Visionary/2IC relationship, I want to briefly share my discovery with you. As I mentioned in the introduction, I was 19 when I married my husband and immediately realized that he had a gambling problem. It took me two years to get help. In those two years, my most significant concern and reason for not doing something about the gambling problem in our family was, "What if my husband stopped gambling? He will be miserable and lose his charm and fun." I was obsessed with worrying about disappointing my partner and who he would turn into if he didn't gamble. In those two years, there was barely ever a moment where I thought, "What about me? How much am I suffering? How much will I pay for the help I need?" When the pain became too much, and there was no fun left in the gambling, I finally walked into my first 12-step meeting.

It was in these meetings that I realized that I, as the spouse of someone with a compulsive personality, is a codependent. I enabled the person next to me to keep doing their destructive work. I covered up for him, filled in, took over, compensated, and at the same time became deeply lonely and resentful, yet controlling and trying to control the situation. If I hid all the money, he wouldn't gamble, etc. But recovery was realizing that I was not in control of him or the outcomes. The only person I am in control of is myself.

I noticed another pattern during my early recovery and working with businesses. I observed many successful business owners and Visionaries have the same compulsive personalities as people with an addiction, yet they are not labeled as addicts. The world is their casino. They flip houses, real estate, and businesses in the name of success, but it is all driven by the addiction to win. There is a constant need for more, never having enough, and the chase for the dopamine high you get when you score. It is even worse for Visionaries and entrepreneurs because they don't have a program to turn to for healing.

Through my years of coaching spouses of people with an addiction, I saw those same patterns again and again. These are patterns of spouses losing their sense of self to "save" their spouse while dealing with deep-rooted resentment.

The starkest discovery was when I became a professional EOS Implementer to help businesses and their leadership teams get healthier. I started noticing those same patterns of enmeshment and loss of self in COOs/Integrators/2ICs. A 2IC would begin with high promises, look capable, and suddenly deteriorate. Some within three months and some within three years, but I have seen it happen too often. I wanted to confirm my discovery, and after much research and experience, the dots lined up.

A significant breakthrough came while reading Dr. Douglas Brackmann's book, *Driven-Understanding and Harnessing the Genetic Gifts Shared by Entrepreneurs, Navy Seals, Pro*

Athletes, and Maybe YOU. He talks about entrepreneurs carrying the D2-D4 gene genetic mutation. He explains how the receptors do not register dopamine hits, and therefore, they are constantly looking for more. That is the crux of addiction and compulsivity.

To better understand compulsivity, we must understand how people decide to act. Usually, a person has a thought that evokes an emotion that prompts them to act. For example, you see a pretty pair of shoes in a store window and think, "Wow, I like that." It evokes the emotion of happiness; you evaluate your feelings, decide if it's worth your action, and then decide to either buy the shoes or continue walking.

People with compulsive personalities have a tough time pausing and evaluating their feelings. They see a pair of shoes, think, "That would look great with my dress," and immediately go and take action. They are not in touch with or bury their emotions; therefore, they take more risks and actions because they don't evaluate outcomes.

Dr. Douglas says, "Driven brains differ in how their reward systems function. The D2 and D4 alleles, mutations present in 8-15% of the population, change nerve receptors, causing them not to fire as easily. Thus, no matter what we do, we don't feel rewarded, at least compared to those who do not have these genetic alleles."

Dr. Douglas also talks about the Narcissistic fantasies of entrepreneurs. A driven Visionary is hyper-focused on their win, which creates tunnel vision. They constantly need that "win." When they have that big house, fancy car, and big business, all will be well in their world; they will be on top and happy. Now it's all lined up.

What Is the Typical DNA of a Visionary?

The typical DNA of a Visionary is somebody who thinks big. They are five steps ahead. They rally people around an idea. They are great at connecting dots. They are great at being creative problem solvers.

In his Inc. article, Justin Breen, founder of Epic F.I.T Network and BrEpic Communications, says, "Visionaries are the most highly functioning dysfunctional people." Most

Visionaries he met have either been bankrupt or close to bankruptcy. They have attention deficit disorder. They deal with depression and learning disabilities. Their need to overcome all of this makes them so highly functional. Traditionally, we look down on such students in the school system. But those are the things that make Visionaries so great. The higher on the scale a Visionary has compulsiveness and ADD, the bigger of a Visionary they are.

Now, their most significant gifts are also their greatest challenge. That is the positive and the negative of being a Visionary. Their compulsiveness creates chaos within organizations because they cannot wait long enough for things to happen. When they see a vision possibly coming into reality, they are onto the next one already. Once, I was working with a Visionary who was struggling with their COO. The 2IC was working slower than he wanted, and I asked him, "When would you want this done?" He said, "The best time would have been yesterday. The next best time would be today." They have zero patience to wait for things to happen.

For example, Brett came to me feeling like he was being micromanaged and controlled. He couldn't understand how, as the 2IC for his company, he was supposed to be the tiebreaker and decision filter if he had no autonomy. Meanwhile, Brett kept feeling like something was wrong with him, that he wasn't doing a good job, and that his confidence was failing. He doubted himself.

By working with me, Brett understood that Visionaries live in the future and want to see constant movement. They are impatient. When he didn't give clear updates to the Visionary about projects and assignments, the Visionary got impatient and started micromanaging because he assumed nothing was getting done.

Brett learned how to communicate concise updates on projects so the Visionary feels heard and sees that things are moving ahead while also asking for his space and needs. Brett learned how to ask that he should not be interrupted with new ideas during focus time so that he can get things done.

What Is the Typical DNA of a 2IC?

The patterns of a relationship dance predict that Visionaries will naturally attract people who are people pleasers, who are the type to enable things to get done and who are detail-oriented, practical, and logical. Therefore, 2ICs are more focused on the immediate future than the far-out future. They like facts and weighing options before taking chances. They have the talent of following through on projects and are hyper-focused on helping others over themselves.

If this is taken to extreme, those types of people end up becoming enmeshed and codependent. Their self-worth is dependent on helping others.

This connection, this dance, this law of inverse attraction, this yin/yang is called "Relationship Math."

What is Relationship Math?

Relationship math comes from Psychologist Ross Rosenberg's book, *The Human Magnetic Syndrome*. Relationship math originates from the concept of the attraction between addicts/narcissists and their significant others.

This is the reflexive attraction between two people in a relationship. It explains how and why opposites attract in relationships and create the magnetic pull in these relationships.

I have tested and proven these concepts countless times, and my informal research has shown that those same concepts apply to the Visionary/2IC relationship.

Ross introduces the idea that every relationship exists with one person being "Self-Focused," and they attract someone "Other-Focused," creating the law of attraction and the human magnetic syndrome that those two types of people will attract each other repeatedly.

Think of the concept of "Self-Focused" versus "Other-Focused" as the difference between the following scenarios. Person number one sees that they might be late for their meeting. They still didn't have their morning coffee. They decide to take the risk of having their coffee and possibly being late because it is essential to their health and well-being and being in a good spirit at the meeting. Person number two sees they might be running five minutes late if they still make a stop to grab their coffee. They decide to forgo their coffee and be on time for the meeting, and while they sit there, they feel resentful and upset that they did not have time to get coffee this morning. Can you relate to any of these two scenarios? This is the difference between a Self-Focused person and an Other-Focused person. A Self-Focused person operates from a place of thinking about themselves and their goals first, while an Other-Focused person puts others first and is concerned about needing to feel needed.

Ross Rosenberg created this continuum to show that to the degree both people in the relationship are equally healthy and unhealthy, they will stay in a magnetic force and not break up. Based on how far each partner is on their side of the spectrum, the degree of the health of their relationship will be determined.

I took the liberty to adapt this to the Visionary/ Second-in-Command relationship.

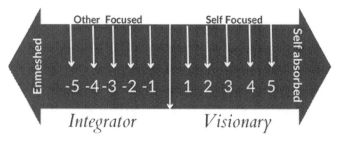

Visionary Integrator Relationship Compatibility Continuums

Other Focused   Self Focused

Enmeshed   -5 -4 -3 -2 -1   1 2 3 4 5   Self absorbed

Integrator   *Visionary*

Based on the Human Magnet Syndrome by Ross Rosenberg LCPC, CADC ©

What is "Self-Focused"?

On the continuum, Visionaries are on the Self-Focused side because of their consistency and similarities with compulsive behavior, which, in the extreme form, leads to self-absorption and narcissism. Now, what that means is they have a strong focus on themselves. They will always think, "How do I present myself to the world?" The writing is literally on the wall. These people build businesses and organizations that are focused on their ideas. Without them, there is no business. You have hundreds of employees focusing on one person's idea.

A Self-Focused person's most significant need is freedom and winning. That is why they created a business in the first place. They want to be free to explore the world without being told what to do. They are constantly running after the narcissistic fantasy of bigger and better. On the other hand, their biggest fear is feeling controlled and losing. Therefore, they are afraid to connect and commit to people because that will cause them to have obligations that feel controlling. They will also push themselves and go as far as self-sabotaging for the need to win.

Think about Steve Jobs and Apple. Think about Elon Musk and Tesla. Without Elon Musk, there is no Tesla. That means the vision is his and is all focused on him. He is focused on himself and rallies people to focus on himself. I have had Visionaries challenge me on this, as one said, "Well, I am such a giving person, and I give so much to others." That is true. I ask that person, "Would you still be comfortable being an employee in your organization and having no say in where the money you are giving is going to? Maybe we will send it to kids in Africa versus helping needy families in Mexico." That person had a look on his face that did not look like it would sit well with him because it was about where he decided his money and contribution would go. That is the idea of being self-relationship-focused. You are focused on your relationship with yourself.

As an EOS implementer, we encourage that the vision should come from the leader. I always say vision comes from the top, and the goal is to align everyone around the Visionary's vision so we can row in one direction and execute effectively. There is nothing inherently wrong with this except that it's a perfect recipe for this dance to happen. Visionaries naturally seek to partner up with people who are the exact opposite of them. That would be people who live to bring others' ideas and visions into reality. They are the helpers of the earth.

What is "Other-Focused"?

Other-Focused people are known as the people who are like the "salt of the earth." The nicest people, many people pleasers, have a hard time saying no. Born from a need to please, they are great at finishing projects. They are great at sorting, organizing, managing details, laying out project plans, and following through. They are Other-Focused. That means they constantly think, "What does the world think of me?" They are very concerned with what people think of them. They have a solid need to be liked and needed. They want to please people and not upset them. They do not like letting down people or disappointing them.

An "Other-Focused" person's most significant need is to feel useful and needed, while their biggest fear is not being needed and not being approved of or not liked. That is why "Other-Focused" people neglect their needs to please others. They will hurt and disappoint themselves just to be liked and wanted.

As a Second-in-Command, do you find yourself helping other leadership team members and the Visionary with their requests and giving them your time before making sure you are covering your own roles and responsibilities, only to find yourself constantly lagging behind, feeling used up and resentful? Skipping breakfast, the gym, saying no to vacations, and family time because you are worried about pleasing the Visionary in your life?

Self-Focused people are wired to seek satisfaction internally, while Other-Focused people will seek satisfaction externally. Self-Focused people look for how they can score a win in every situation, and Other-focused people constantly look for validation from others.

Self-Focused people will quickly judge others versus themselves. They constantly think, "That person is such a jerk; why are they so stupid? Why don't they get it?" Other-Focused people tend to be very harsh on themselves and constantly judge themselves, thinking, "This guy must be thinking I am such a jerk; I am so stupid."

Self-Focused people avoid attachment and don't get too close and comfortable, while Other-Focused people anxiously attach and constantly want interactions with their partners.

Self-Focused people lack empathy; they have difficulty consistently thinking about others, getting out of their tunnel vision that leads to their big win, and taking a minute to think,

"Wait, what do others feel or need?" If you tell them to do something that involves taking care of others, they have a hard time doing that consistently.

A Visionary who is Self-Focused will often not innately take into consideration other people's preferences and needs. If they like dry red wine, they assume everyone does. If an employee complains and says they are unsatisfied with their role, the Visionary will try to fix it with what they believe they would want instead of getting curious and asking the person what would make them happy. If a Visionary's focus is money, they assume it's everyone's focus. They will give the person a raise without pausing to consider anything else that might bother the employee. When the employee complains again, the Visionary will think, "Why is he/she complaining? I just gave them a raise," when the employee's main concern wasn't more money; they just wanted to be heard and wanted more compassion or accommodation.

On the other hand, Other-Focused people might have too much empathy and be enmeshed. They sincerely care about others and empathize to the degree that it can disrupt their life, and they feel everyone's feelings but their own.

Suppose they know an employee is in a challenging personal relationship. In that case, they might get too involved in trying to fix the employee's problems, hoping it will help that person perform better at work. They become distracted and overworked, then underperform in their role and get entangled, expending energy instead of focusing on holding people accountable and ensuring the business functions properly.

Once you recognize this pattern, you will realize it in relationships: Visionaries and 2ICs; husbands and wives; mothers and children.

The Dance

You will notice that one side of the continuum is marked as positive numbers, and one side is marked as negative numbers. That is because, in a magnetic relationship, each partner's differences cancel each other out, effectively bringing the equation to zero-sum. This is the law of inverse attraction and attracting people who are at your emotional health level. The positive and negative force in a battery creates electricity. An extremely unhealthy Visionary will attract an equally extremely unhealthy 2IC, and they will get stuck in this "dance." This means that if you have a highly self-absorbed Visionary, they will usually attract a highly enmeshed COO, and a more center-focused Visionary will attract a more center-focused 2IC.

We all know those stuck in a job, position, or marriage that they don't like, yet they don't leave. That is because they are caught in a magnetic force. Whether you find yourself at the extreme side of the continuum or in the center, the relationship is functional to a degree if both partners are equally on the opposite side of the spectrum. This doesn't mean it is healthy and maximized for the business or each other, but it is functional nevertheless. You catch each other and balance each other out.

The Range

The degree of being Self-Relationship-Focused and Other Relationship-Focused runs on a scale from 0-5, representing how healthy the person is. The closer a person is to the center, the zero, the more they are situation and center-focused and have a healthy sense of self and others. They can consider their needs and other's needs, prioritize and differentiate what is important, set boundaries, and be in touch with their self-care and needs while being assertive to others.

On one side of the spectrum is the very Self-Focused Visionary; on the other side, there is a very enmeshed Other-Focused Second-In-Command.

Let's explore the entire range of Self-Focused Visionaries. Try to think about what a very healthy Visionary looks like. Visionaries need to have Self-Focus to build and innovate businesses.

On the other hand, we will explore the range of Other-Focused 2ICs. Look carefully at what a very enmeshed 2IC versus a healthy center-focused 2IC looks like. We need Other-Focused people to bring visions into reality to execute and follow through. There is nothing wrong with being self or Other-Focused. The goal is to find the perfect balance to create a healthy, productive relationship where no one feels used and unseen.

Self-Relationship-Oriented Visionary Spectrum

This orientation scale ranges from the most self-absorbed to the amicable, interdependent balance.

The most self-absorbed Visionary type is a 5, and the healthiest have a healthy perspective of others at a 1.

5 An Extreme Self-Relationship-Oriented Visionary

At the highest degree, a five, is highly selfish. They possess a massive sense of entitlement. They exploit people to get them to do what they want. They lack empathy. They need excessive admiration. It is always about them and their ideas. They have an inflated sense of self, and they need special treatment.

4 A Highly Self-Centered Visionary

At the fourth degree, Visionaries are highly self-centered, often seeking personal glory and recognition. They may listen to others but prioritize their ideas and agendas over collaborative efforts. They still expect special treatment and a "pass."

3 A Moderately Self-Focused Visionary

At the third degree, Visionaries have some self-awareness but still consistently see things through the lens of "what's the win for me here?" They may occasionally consider the contributions and needs of others but remain primarily self-driven. They have a hard time consistently caring for others.

2 A Balanced Visionary

At the second degree, a balanced Visionary strikes a reasonable equilibrium between self-orientation and consideration of others. They can handle not being first and not talking first and listening instead. They value collaboration and recognize the importance of collective success.

1 An Amicable Visionary

At the first degree, they are characterized by their strong self-awareness, which means they can look outside their bubble and see the world from other people's perspectives. They can stop and think, "I wonder how my 2IC sees this?" They have a genuine concern for the well-being and the contribution of others. They are more interested in understanding others than being understood. They actively foster a collaborative environment and prioritize collective achievements.

You will notice that the healthier a Visionary becomes, the more empathetic and self-aware they are about their strengths and weaknesses and know how to include and be considerate of others.

Other-Relationship-Oriented 2IC Spectrum

This orientation scale ranges from the most enmeshed to the healthiest, interdependent balance.

The most enmeshed Second-In-Command type is a -5, and the healthiest have a healthy interdependence at a -1.

-5 An Extremely Enmeshed Other-Relationship-Oriented 2IC

At the -5 degree, 2ICs will exhibit total codependence and are wholly entangled with others and the organization. They have no sense of individuation and an inability to differentiate their needs and feelings from others. They are not in touch with their priorities and boundaries, giving up too much time to others either by doing work others are supposed to be doing or listening to petty complaints. This makes them highly susceptible to manipulation and devalues them. As a way of protecting themselves to try to reclaim themselves desperately, they often turn into highly manipulative people, using self-pity as a form of control.

These 2ICs struggle to make decisions independently; they constantly seek the Visionary's validation and approval before making decisions. They are worried about being useful rather than impactful and effective. They tend to overthink and overcomplicate. They are afraid to hold people accountable because they fear conflict. They feel too much for others, are "too nice" and overly kind, which ends up happening is that they hurt the business and people in the interim, which makes them unkind to the people who matter the most. They are very focused on the Visionary, constantly putting them on a pedestal, making them untouchable instead of focusing on the company's greater good. That is like feeding the addiction instead of putting down boundaries to enable the person to heal. They are not in touch with their needs and desires and care poorly for themselves. This, in turn, makes them feel resentful, alone, and abandoned.

-4 A Highly Enmeshed 2IC

At the -4 degree, the 2IC is highly enmeshed and struggles to assert themselves. They prioritize others' needs to an extreme degree, which makes them passive-aggressive or controlling. They have difficulty identifying their feelings and often need others to comfort them. They may suffer from burnout due to over-commitment to the Visionary's agenda. They try to hold people accountable, but in the struggle to do it assertively, they may come across as dominant and controlling or the opposite as a victim and enabler. They often prioritize the Visionaries' whims over the organization's actual needs because they are afraid to push back. They have difficulty asserting themselves and come across as very aggressive when they finally muster the courage to express their needs or opinions. They cannot consistently take care of their own needs while helping others.

-3 A Moderate Other Focused 2IC

At the -3 degree, the 2IC is moderately enmeshed and exhibits moderate codependency tendencies. They value teamwork but struggle to pay more attention to their well-being and needs. They still need to work on setting boundaries and prioritizing themselves, recognizing their strengths, and how they can maximize their strengths in their role. They often doubt themselves, their needs, and their abilities, still seeking validation and confirmation from the Visionary and leadership team. They can hold their team accountable to a degree, yet they struggle not to put the Visionary on a pedestal. They are sometimes successful at being assertive. It is a constant, exhausting, and balancing act between discerning their feelings, needs, and wants from others and which ones to prioritize.

-2 A Balanced 2IC

At the -2 degree, the 2IC is balanced and maintains a healthy interdependence between self and others. They don't constantly need others to validate their emotions and can identify when they feel burnt out or resentful. They still want to be needed and liked, but they can assert themselves appropriately and collaborate effectively without losing their sense of self. They can somewhat handle criticism and objection. They can prioritize and make decisions without constantly looking for the Visionary's approval. They don't often focus on pleasing the people around them and can be assertive. They still find themselves sometimes exhausted and burnt out, reminding themselves to care for themselves.

-1 An Effective 2IC

At the -1 degree, the 2IC is centered and situation-focused. With a strong sense of balance, they understand the importance of both self-care and teamwork. They know that if they neglect themselves, everyone suffers, and if they utilize their energy in the wrong places or get stuck in the minutia, it doesn't benefit the organization. They can balance their needs and their organization's goals, fostering a harmonious and productive environment. They are in touch with their leadership style and have confidence in their skills. They are great at delegating because they don't have a strong need to be needed.

They have the skills to facilitate healthy conversations because they are not afraid of conflict and don't get unnecessarily enmeshed and involved with others. They don't take on other people's work and instead hold people accountable in a pleasant, loving way.

They are pleasant to be around and not overly critical of themselves or others. They are great at discerning where their expertise is needed, have a developed sense of intuition, and can handle pivoting when the situation requires or facts change.

Becoming Balanced

In the book, *How to Be Second*, authors Nathan Young and David Hartman discuss healthy versus unhealthy followership and how subservience doesn't serve anyone: the Visionary, 2IC, or the organization.

He describes unhealthy followership as being subservient versus willing to serve. It is not constantly questioning what is good; it is about being discerning. "I was just following orders", is not something that a Second needs to be saying, is what the authors explain.

You need to own your decisions.

Young & Hartman further expound how "Healthy Seconds enjoy a trusting reciprocal relationship with the Visionary; they can build solutions to problems and have ready access to data to make decisions and improvements; their superior listens to potential solutions that a second generates and ensures that the solutions have fidelity to the original vision". They continue to explain "healthy seconds seek to buy in, but do not lead by consensus and will delicately tread the line between proposing solutions and imposing solutions". This description of a healthy second perfectly describes a 2IC at the -2 or -1 on the spectrum.

This quote highlights the law of inverse attraction at play and aligns with the spectrum outlined above. "An unhealthy second may have chosen to follow someone who is non-communicative".

An unhealthy second will go down rabbit holes on facts, inhibiting them from making decisions, teasing apart systems and processes, and become personally judgmental. They will begin to undermine leadership and fail to be objective, constructive, and optimistic.

Why is Being a Balanced, Center-Focused Integrator Important?

Let's discuss why it's essential and beneficial for a Second-In-Command to become more center-focused and, if not, how it affects you and the business.

Let's paint a picture of what unhealthy enmeshment does to a 2IC and the business. A highly Self-Focused Visionary can affect the 2IC with emotional distress, low self-esteem, burnout, creativity suppression, and job dissatisfaction. They are arrogant and not pleasant to be around, causing employees to leave and not trust leadership in the company.

Since this book is about COOs, I want to focus on the effects of an entangled 2IC. This 2IC is not assertive, does not have a sense of self, and does not put their needs and priorities in the correct order. This causes self-neglect, excessive codependency, and lack of autonomy. They avoid confluence. They over-adapt, meaning they don't have an intact filter radar. They don't tap into their gift of discernment and intuition or discern good from wrong ideas and direction. They miss opportunities to pivot and expand, which can be a huge detriment to the organization.

They are constantly over-adapting to the Visionary and the environment.

What is the effect on the business and the Visionary? They limit the challenges to the Visionary and provide little constructive challenge or alternative viewpoints to the Visionary's ideas. Meaning they become overly agreeable instead of a collaborative challenger. This can result in a lack of critical thinking and potential oversight of essential factors. With innovation, the organization may be able to innovate and adapt to changing market conditions. When the 2IC overly conforms to the Visionary's vision, innovative ideas from the 2IC may be suppressed. They risk burnout, impacting long-term effectiveness and well-being. This can result in disruptions to project timelines and outcomes. Worst of all, they create dependency on themselves.

The Visionary may become overly dependent on the COO for support and execution. They are creating a bottleneck. They are becoming the chokepoint in decision-making and project management. This creates an unhealthy power dynamic. The extreme or other relationship-oriented 2IC can inadvertently reinforce an unhealthy power dynamic, where the Visionary holds significant control and influence over the COO's decisions and actions. This greatly reduces accountability. A lack of assertiveness and conflict avoidance can lead to reduced accountability within the organization. They are preventing issues and challenges from being addressed more openly.

They risk the long-term sustainability of the organization and its adaptability. This may be at risk if the 2IC consistently prioritizes the immediate satisfaction of others over strategic planning and problem-solving. They are pleasing the Visionary rather than serving the organization's greater good. The organization may experience delays and inefficiencies in decision-making due to the 2IC's constant need for approval and guidance from the Visionary. We all agree that Visionaries have difficulty letting go of the vine and giving up control of the day-to-day details of the business. Visionaries may need help delegating effectively, and they rely heavily on 2ICs to support them. However, the 2ICs may also need help to delegate effectively because 2ICs can easily get trapped in the need to help others and feel useful. This can limit both of their capabilities to take on new initiatives.

For example, Theresa, an Integrator for an engineering company of 30 employees, reached out to me, saying she was feeling burnt out and resentful. She's constantly jumping from one thing to the next, playing wack-a-mole because she feels that as a 2IC, she needs to be there for everyone to keep it all together, but then she can't get any of her own jobs done.

When she took the Empowered COO assessment, she realized that her score of a -4 meant she was too busy pleasing and not serving. She felt undeserving of her promotion as Integrator and, therefore, felt like she needed to compensate by pleasing the leadership team and constantly helping them with things that they were really accountable for and that they were just shirking onto her.

After working with Theresa for a few months, she admitted that remembering to empower herself and be assertive is a daily struggle, but she wouldn't go back to her old self for any money. Now she knows her limits, is confident in her work, and therefore is delivering more, making everyone around her so much happier.

Exceptions to Relationship Math

Keep in mind that partners and Fractional Integrators are exceptions to the rules of Relationship Math.

The concept of "Fractional COOs/Integrators" has lately become a "thing". I want to highlight an important factor without discussing if it works or doesn't. Perhaps one of the reasons Fractional Integrators have become so attractive to Visionaries is because they are not "married to the business." They don't get enmeshed, are transparent with their boundaries, and act more in control, like they are driving the bus. The Fractional Integrator sets the terms and conditions for the engagement, leaving less room for overstepping boundaries and creating dysfunction in the relationship. Deep down, every Visionary appreciates that because it takes extra effort for Visionaries to be accommodating, so they are relieved when someone is assertive and comes forth with the terms and conditions.

From what I have seen in comparison to full-time Integrators, fractional Integrators much more often exhibit assertiveness, decisiveness, and discernment, the key ingredients to being an effective, high-level Integrator. They don't get comfortable and complacent in their seat because their engagement is usually short and constantly evaluated. If I had to guess, fractional Integrators probably have more entrepreneurial spirit than traditional Integrators. They are more comfortable with risks since they must always be on the lookout for their next opportunity.

On the Kolbe assessment (an assessment that evaluates your "MO" the way you approach challenges and projects, Fractional Integrators come in higher in "quick start. You can read more about Kolbe at Kolbe.com.

Because of everything mentioned above, it is rare to find fractional Integrators becoming enmeshed and losing themselves while working with Visionaries. Perhaps it is time for

Integrators and COOs to start acting like Fractional COOs.

With all that being said about fractional Integrators, in an ideal world, I wish "Short engagement Integrators" would be a concept over "Fractional Integrators." I believe it is difficult and almost impossible for one to fully immerse themselves into a business, hold people accountable, and be a true supportive role when you are just tapping in once a week and juggling five different engagements at once. I think Fractional Integrators would be able to bring way more value by fully immersing themselves into an engagement for a short period of time – 3-6 months while building a path for succession.

The same goes for business partnerships where one partner is the Visionary and the other the Integrator. Because both are equally financially invested in the business, there is this constant pull to move the business forward and a higher risk tolerance. Yet the stake in the company can also be used as a bargaining and power chip, which a traditional Integrator does not have. The relationship doesn't have a "magnetic pull," meaning each partner is not afraid to step away since they own a piece of the pie.

For all these reasons, partners are less on the opposite side of the "relationship continuum" and, therefore, are less likely to get entangled with each other, where one becomes highly Self-Focused and the other extremely Other-Focused because they are wired to look out for their best interests constantly.

A Personal Note to You, the 2IC

I want to acknowledge that reading this spectrum can feel emotionally draining and hard. You might think, "This author has no idea what she is talking about; this is not me." If that is you, that is ok. Close this book and continue with your life.

But if you find yourself thinking, "Wow, I had no idea I am this enmeshed". If you have no idea why you are feeling resentful, out of touch with yourself, and burnt out. If you look in the mirror and see an unrecognizable shadow of yourself, then you have just done the most challenging work. The first step is becoming aware. Bravo to you.

I invite you and warn you at the same time. Healing and moving towards becoming center-focused creates a shift and imbalance in your Visionary/Integrator relationship. You are about to break that magnetic energy and dance. What can happen is either one of two things. Nature abhors a vacuum, so nature will force balance to be restored. The best-case scenario is that the Visionary in your life follows your lead and, unbeknown to themselves, starts changing because human beings are mirrors; we gravitate and mirror behaviors we see.

Or you might decide that you no longer want to be stuck in this exhausting magnetic energy, and it is time to move on.

Take a minute, pause, and breathe. Decide if you want to turn the page to the next chapter because it might be the most ambitious yet gratifying journey you have ever been on to EMPOWER yourself.

They say, "Be careful what you wish for because it might happen."

I am excited for you! for this journey to unfold because I know that you deserve to be your best-empowered self at every moment, in every role.

Take the online empowerment assessment to see where you are on the spectrum: **www.empoweredcoo.com/assessment**

Questions to Think About:

Where do you identify yourself on the relationship continuum?

Where is the Visionary on the relationship continuum?

How does understanding the spectrum clarify your relationship?

Can you remember a point in time when you gave up your self-care to please the Visionary?

Can you identify a time when you were afraid of conflict and chose to "keep the peace" instead, but it ended up not serving anyone?

How do you think you, the Visionary, and the organization will benefit from you moving more towards being Center-Focused?

PART TWO

Chapter Five

What Is the Secret Sauce of an Empowered COO?

Before we move on and show you how you can empower yourself as a Second-in-Command and right-hand hand to any Visionary, I want to make it abundantly clear that there is nothing wrong with being an "Other-Focused" person. You aren't less than or defective. You are unique, and the world needs you and your strengths so that you are at your best, to help Visionaries bring their dreams into reality.

When you are an empowered, Other-Focused person, you are great at following through on projects and can tune into other people's needs. You can listen to what's not being said and are able to tap into your intuition, be discerning, sort ideas, and prioritize needs and projects.

To recap what the 2IC or Integrator roles are, Gino Wickman and Mark C. Winters describe it as:

- Lead, manage, and hold people accountable
- Business plan and execution/P&L Results
- Integrate major functions
- Resolving cross-functional issues
- Communication across the organization.

Again, I cannot urge you enough to check out www.Rocketfueluniversity.com and all its resources to learn more. It is a pre-requisite to do the work that will follow here.

To do all of the above, you must be an Empowered 2IC.

An Empowered 2IC is like a triage nurse. When a trauma patient comes in, you assess situations quickly, determine a plan of action, see the necessary steps in your mind's eye, direct and delegate, and make it happen. You are strong and assertive and do not lose yourself under pressure or in times of crisis.

An Empowered COO has:

- A strong self-identity

- Great communication skills

- Understands and is in touch with their leadership style

- Has confidence in their skills

- Is an encouraging leader

- Models leadership and management skills

- Manages conflict well

- Can discern and filter ideas effectively

- Is independent and self-reliant

- Has good self-care skills

- Is focused on serving and not pleasing

- Keeps pace with the Visionary and contributes by executing the vision.

So how do you get all that?

These roles are soft skills, which you usually don't learn in college, school, or regular job training. At the root, these soft skills can be summed up as

- Project management skills,

- People and emotional intelligence skills

- Strategic thinking skills

Giving Up the Need to Control

Before I share with you the secret sauce of a successful 2IC that is center and situation-focused, I must share with you the underpinnings of what causes someone to get higher on the scale of enmeshment. The root cause is the need to control. When you were put into the Integrator seat, you were essentially given the pass to become "Chief Control Freak." After all, it is your job to make sure the trains run on time. It is natural to assume that the way to keep things in control is to exert control. But as you have seen in the previous chapter, having a strong need to be needed, to please and get things done, causes just the opposite: An extreme loss of control of yourself. You might have "control" over the situation, but you lose all control of YOU.

Therefore, the first step to becoming center-focused and back in touch with yourself is giving up the need to control. Resigning to the fact that you only possess finite, limited efforts, and at the end of the day, some decisions and outcomes are just not in your hands. Accept your limitations in order to free yourself. Stop trying to fix, solve, and change the Visionary as a person. You won't make them less demanding, unrealistic, and driven. Many times before, you have tried, but no one has succeeded. That is the Driven Visionary's personal journey, and no one can do it for them. Instead, appreciate the fire they bring to your water, their uniqueness, and how essential they are to the vitality of the organization. Appreciate that you can complement them as the missing piece but not change them. Do not treat them like a broken toy. Recognize your differences and honor each other for it.

The Visionary/Integrator spectrum in the previous chapter is the perfect depiction of your differences in mindset and wiring. Integrators tend to work from a past mindset, looking at data and past results, oftentimes getting stuck in the past. Visionaries tend to live in the future. Planning, dreaming, and often forgetting about the present. Forgetting to appreciate and focus on the present. It is the work of the Visionary and Integrator to become more present, situation and center-focused. That is the work you will learn in the rest of the book.

The Secret Sauce

The secret sauce to being an Empowered Integrator/Second-In-Command is gaining a healthier sense of self, which means moving closer to being "Center-Focused." That means developing what I call "ADD" Assertiveness, Decisiveness, and Discernment.

Assertiveness means moving from passive/aggressive communication to assertive and excellent facilitation/mediation skills. Say what you mean and mean what you say.

Decisiveness is having a confident sense of self, solid boundaries, knowledge of your wants, needs and preferences, and the ability to relate requests confidently.

Discernment is having a keen intuition, skills to filter good from bad, and being focused on prioritizing.

Questions to Think About:

Do you feel like you need to control situations and outcomes in order to be an effective COO?

Can you imagine a world where you let go?

How would you rate your communication skills?

Are you uncomfortable with conflict?

Do you have a hard time feeling deserving?

Chapter Six
What Is Assertiveness?

Assertiveness is the ability to state your needs and stand your ground while acknowledging and giving empathy to another person's needs and then doing what is best for the situation. You must mean what you say and say what you mean.

- Assertiveness is having excellent communication skills.

- Learning to speak what I call "Visionary language" so you can get through to the Visionary and be on the same page, get things done, and move the organization forward.

- It is about developing excellent conflict management skills so you can be an expert communicator across all functions of the organization. Most importantly, it is about being a mediator between the Visionary and leadership team.

You Deserve It!

The first step is to feel worthy. Stand up tall! You can only be assertive when you deeply feel deserving.

Reading this, I know you might feel a pit in your stomach. That is because other-relationship-oriented people carry a lot of fear and shame about prioritizing themselves.

This might mean that you need to do the work to explore those messages of fear and shame. Ask yourself, "Where does this come from? Who said that I do not deserve to prioritize myself, know my needs, and have self-awareness about what I am feeling while I am feeling it?" Get in touch with your needs and feelings. This will make you more assertive. Perhaps, get a personal coach who understands the challenges of codependency. It will be a giant step in the direction of becoming more assertive, and creating a healthy sense of self and interdependence.

The Four Styles of Communication

There are four ways humans communicate.

- Passive

- Aggressive

- Passive/Aggressive

- Assertive

Let's explore these types and see why it is so essential to develop assertive communication as a Second-in-Command.

Passive Communication

Passive communication is all about what you are NOT saying. Staying silent but brooding is passive communication. Your body language is communicating while you are being verbally silent. Being passive is about expecting people to know your needs without you expressing them. Are you expecting people to read your mind?

Being passive is about denying your needs because you fear upsetting the Visionary and or leadership team. You choose to forgo your preferences or what you think is right for the sake of "keeping the peace."

You are essentially teaching people it is ok to mistreat you because you are not speaking up for yourself.

Aggressive Communication

Aggressive communication is voicing demands in a non-negotiable way and being insensitive to others' opinions, feelings, or needs. It is a way of forcing the other party to do what you want them to do with the narrative of helping them because that is your given "role," and you are desperately trying to execute and make it happen. Aggressive communication can look like backhanded compliments, procrastination, withdrawal, refusal to communicate, or being very controlling, saying things like "I said what I said, I won't repeat myself" and "You're out of your mind if you think that will work."

"Can you do anything right?"

I have seen Visionaries become incapacitated and businesses stagnate because the 2IC has resorted to such an over-controlling stance or dynamic. When Other-Focused (or the highest level of Self-Focused) people reach the end of their rope, they can turn aggressive.

Passive/Aggressive Communication

Passive/Aggressive communication is a consistent pattern of not expressing negative feelings verbally. Instead of honest and direct communication, passive/aggressive is about body language that is aggressive, like eye-rolling or shrugging, while verbally being passive, like saying "whatever" and going with the flow. Many Integrators tend to be passive or passive-aggressive in their communication because they are afraid to speak up for themselves and speak their true minds. You might be afraid of losing your job. You might fear disapproval and not being liked. Remember, an "Other-Focused" person's highest need is to feel needed and respected as a nice/kind person. Therefore, they will hold it all in and burst when it reaches the brim. Or subtly voice their thoughts and opinions in backhanded ways.

Pretending that you don't care while boiling inside is a good example. Another example of being passive/aggressive is accepting decisions with a shrug while knowing that it is not for the good of the company. When you feel that your needs don't matter or that you don't have an opinion, you are sliding into passive/aggressive mode.

This style of communication reduces tension and avoids conflicts in the short-term. You may breathe a sigh of relief, but in the long-run, you are left feeling misunderstood, unheard, and then resentful.

Examples of passive communication are saying things like "Whatever you want, I don't care", "Whatever the team decides," and "I don't have an opinion (when you do)." Saying these passive statements while feeling angry inside is an indirect way to express negative feelings. The anger and aggressiveness spill out in other ways. Therefore, there is usually a disconnect between what a passive/aggressive person verbally says and what they actually do.

Their communication may be sprinkled with sarcasm, snide remarks, dodging, or sulking when things start going awry. It is a consistent pattern of denying their emotion of anger or helplessness.

Passive aggressive communication is frequent apologizing while asking for something you need.

Saying, "Here we go again..." Saying, "I guess there's nothing I can do about it." Loud sighing.

Saying, "I wish it weren't always me having to hold everyone accountable." Shrugging and saying, "That's fine, I guess."

Body language also plays a massive part in communication. Rolling eyes and shoulder shrugging are examples that I often see with 2ICs who half-heartedly agree to a plan but don't commit.

Assertive Communication

Assertive communication is about saying what you mean and meaning what you say. It is a direct style and includes openly sharing feelings and needs while leaving space and understanding others. Assertive communication is respectful of other people's feelings and needs. When using this style of communication, a large amount of time is spent on listening and hearing the other party. When speaking or sharing an opinion, it is said firmly and without hesitation. The other party can feel that you are unwavering, but they will still feel heard and respected.

You stand up for yourself and uphold your boundaries with kindness and compassion. You respect other people's boundaries, and you are willing to compromise or collaborate if needed.

With assertive communication, you worry less about being liked and nice and more about being kind.

Assertive communication looks like:

- "I am currently finishing up a few urgent and important tasks. Once those are wrapped up, I will have time next week to help you. Will that work for you?"

- "I can see that, but I'd like to…"

- "I am concerned that the project will be at risk if we do not meet this deadline. I need us to brainstorm a way to make it happen."

- "It appears that we disagree on this point. Let's find a solution we can work with to get us the desired results."

How Can You Achieve Assertive Communication?

There are thousands of books and resources on building communication tools. Here are some tools that are especially helpful for someone learning to become more assertive.

1. Don't Deflect Your Needs and Feelings

Deflecting emotions is when you project what you are feeling on others and claim it is their feeling, while all along, it is yours.

It is common for Other-Focused people to get caught up in deflecting without recognizing that they are doing so. This prevents you from being in touch with yourself and what you feel and want, and, therefore, you may become passive-aggressive.

For example, if a COO wants compensation for holiday time off, they might say, "Everyone in the office is upset because they want to be paid for time off." This is you projecting your feelings on others instead of owning what you feel.

Deflecting can look like getting annoyed and upset at someone for being late, being a perfectionist or being lazy. In reality, you are feeling guilty for not training that person properly or hiring the wrong person. You bounce your own uncomfortable feeling away in order to avoid it by painting a situation differently than it is. It doesn't feel good to admit feeling like a failure or feeling guilty. So, instead, you deflect your anger and shame onto others.

2. Active Listening

There are so many great resources out there on active listening. Chris Voss, author of "Never Split the Difference," calls it tactical empathy. Being a Second-In-Command involves developing extraordinary listening skills. You must listen to people's emotions, motives, and what is being said and not said, as well as the underlying feelings.

Tactical empathy includes becoming an expert in mirroring back to people what they said, getting curious, and asking great questions.

John Bradshaw, author of many books, says active listening is "listening for congruence. Congruence matches up content and process. Does his body match his words?" Do you understand this person and his MO? Can you get through to them?

3. Use I Statements

Get used to being comfortable with using "I" statements. I need, I want, I think, etc. Part of becoming empowered and assertive is getting comfortable with having needs, wants, and requests. Don't talk in plural form.

In my experience in working with "Other-Focused" people, I notice that they tend to use a lot of plural language when they mean themselves. This stems from the pressure of living the persona of being someone who serves others and doesn't have personal needs.

4. The Most Important Question

Most importantly, when you find yourself in a situation where you catch yourself being passive/aggressive, take a moment to ask yourself the most crucial question: "What Do I Want?"

I know this might sound silly and simple, but I cannot tell you how many times I ask 2ICs, "What do you want?" they tell me, "Wow, I never thought of that." They can tell me what the Visionary wants, what the team wants, and what the lawyer and general manager wants, but they never stop to ask themselves, "What do I want?"

Your worth is not based on how much you produce, what family you were born into, and your current skill level. You have what it takes to learn how to be assertive. Start by asking yourself, "What do I want?"

5. Being "Nice" Versus "Kind"

Are you nice? Are you kind? A big mistake that Other-Focused people make is confusing 'nice' with 'kind.' Consistently, being nice hurts people in the long run. Embodying kindness is about taking the medicine; even though it tastes horrible, you know it's for the best.

Being nice is all about not saying what you are thinking because you are afraid you'll hurt someone's feelings. Being kind is about saying what needs to be said assertively. Saying it in a way that the other party can be receptive to constructive criticism and help them be a better employee.

Questions to Think About:

Do you struggle with being an Assertive communicator?

Do you feel worthy of voicing your needs?

Do you find it difficult to identify your feelings and needs?

What is your #1 need right now?

What is one assertive message you want to try and communicate?

Chapter Seven
How to Speak Visionary

Originally, this book was titled *How to Speak to Visionaries so They Listen and How to Listen, so that You Are on the Same Page*, but then it spiraled into so much more, and I am glad it did. At the root of learning to speak Visionary is understanding the root of their identity. And if there is only ONE thing that you take away from this book, I want it to be this:

Visionaries are goal-focused and driven by a need for freedom and winning. This is the sum of their identity.

This one sentence defines Visionaries. It encompasses all aspects of the Driven gene that author Dr. Douglas Brackmann defined. It is mentioned earlier in this book and is worth repeating again and again. Repeat it till you remember it.

Visionaries are goal-focused and driven by a need for freedom and winning.

Visionaries have short attention spans and a need for speed.

You want people to honor your identity. Can you see how imperative it is to honor the Visionary's identity?

When you understand what drives someone, you can speak to them in their language. If you understand that a Visionary's innate drive is winning and freedom, you can center all your communication around that, and it will strike gold. If you can keep the essential definition of a Visionary in mind while you talk to a Visionary, you will end up on the winning side. You will be their collaborator instead of their challenger and enemy. Since visionaries perceive anything standing in the way of their goals as an obstacle, it is easy for them to quickly see their Second–in-Command as an obstacle rather than collaboration.

Do you want to experience the Visionary learning and listening in places and ideas that you have always been struggling with? Let me show you how it can work.

Visionaries become business owners because they feel shackled and boxed in. They may have been mistreated by a previous employer – which fueled their need for freedom. A Visionary saw a need or innovation where they could do something better, faster, smarter, igniting their drive to win. Perhaps, they were working and told themselves, "I could do it better. I do not want to be told what to do." They opened their own business because nobody would tell them what to do. They love a good win, whether it means a competition, figuring out something that seems impossible, or breaking a ceiling; this is what excites them.

But suddenly, their business is growing, and they hire an Integrator or 2IC. Now, they are being told what to do. They are the antithesis of conformation, and when you ask them to conform, it triggers them. It causes a childlike reaction. Each of us has personal triggers, and when you are in a trusting, committed relationship, knowing each other's triggers is important.

As a Second-In-Command, you are driven by wanting to make things happen. Yet, you often get stuck because you need the Visionary to buy-in so that you can move forward. You are at the mercy of getting the Visionary to cooperate.

Remember that you are not resistant to systems and processes. You welcome them. You like order. You are driven by data and the past, while visionaries are driven with an eye and pulse on the future. However, Visionaries struggle with systems and processes because they feel it confines them. Many claim it prevents their creative energy from flowing. When you think, "I am going to give my Visionary an agenda. I will show them exactly which booths to visit or what to say at a meeting." Visionaries will perceive it as, "You are trying to control me. You are trying to tell me what I need to do."

If you make the Visionary feel like you are forcing or controlling them, it will automatically trigger a negative response in them because it will restrict their need for freedom. For example, if you need the Visionary to show up at a certain place at a certain time, telling him he needs to show up is making him feel controlled. How can you give him freedom while working well together?

Here are some tips I compiled that will help you honor the Visionary's identity while creating synergy and buy-in.

NO Oriented Questions.

Being able to say NO feels very empowering. Chris Voss, author of *Never Split the Difference*, teaches the concept of No-oriented questions as a negotiation tool. It is asking questions in a way where the best answer would be a no. For example: "Would it be a bad idea if we had a quick 15-minute meeting in the morning to get on the same page before you start your day?" you phrase the question in a way that the entrepreneur doesn't have to do much thinking and their brain automatically goes to "No, that would not be a bad idea" or if it would be a bad idea, they will right away tell you why.

Getting to the Next YES

As Integrators, we want a yes to the whole project or a yes to tabling the whole idea. But sometimes, the best way to get buy-in to a commitment, project, or idea is to just get them to the next immediate yes. Let's say there is a project that you need to work on. The first yes would be, "Can you sit down with me to discuss this project?" If they say yes to that, you are one step closer. Then the next question is, "Can we spend X amount of time talking about the first portion, and then the rest we will spend discussing your idea on it?" They say yes to that. Then, you slowly walk from one yes to the next instead of getting a whole yes.

NO Can Be A Cop Out

If you are recovering from codependence, it is important to learn to say an assertive no, when appropriate. Sometimes, a flat-out no, does not gain buy-in and cooperation.

I believe that oftentimes, saying "no" to an idea or request is a cop-out. As COOs, we feel we have to say no a lot, but that isn't true. If you have the right discernment and communication skills, you rarely ever have to be the "Bad Guy" and say no. A little secret: Most ideas Visionaries conceptualize, if they don't have the who and the network, it has a poor chance of execution because a classic Visionary is not high on follow through.

When they attempt to create change solo, it causes chaos and has a short shelf life. For example, if a Visionary wants to implement a "No phone rule" at meetings. How long would it last if there was not anyone taking it to the next level, creating a lock box or some kind of incentive for this idea?

As a 2IC, you most probably feel that you constantly must rein in the Visionary, so you quickly resort to just saying "no." This is where the art of breaking down ideas is so valuable.

This also involves the skill of discernment. What you can do instead is get the Visionary to see the idea from a place where they themselves veto it. This takes getting curious and not hysterical right away. It is about asking great questions.

Picture this: A Visionary walks into your office and says, "I looked at the numbers. I want to double our sales by next year". Of course, being the more realistic one, you get a knee-jerk reaction. Your brain right away screams, "NOOOO." Getting curious is saying, "That is an interesting idea; tell me more". The Visionary says, "We will need more equipment, more employees, more salespeople, more product, but it's doable. I am telling you I can get more machines up and running within a month." This is where you use active listening skills, like mirroring and labeling to show the Visionary that you are interested, engaged, and want to understand more. You might ask, "Up and running in a month? I know getting machines delivered usually takes 8-10 months minimum". Now, you gently forced the Visionary to come back in touch with reality. They respond, "Oh, right. That is an issue." Now, the Visionary must really think this through.

You see, Visionaries are always 10 steps ahead, which is a good thing, but it can also be a detriment because they forget to address what is right in front of them in reality. This is how you keep navigating this conversation until you get to the root or a conclusion that works for everyone and makes sense. You might say, "Okay, do you want to work on placing the order for machines to be here in 8-10 months?" That might mean taking one small step in the direction of the goal the Visionary is looking for and breaking down the plan to a more feasible goal. Now, you become a collaborator and not an antagonizer.

Create Buy In

What is buy-in? It is commitment. These tools work amazingly with leadership teams as well as Visionaries. How do you get someone to commit to a decision? Patrick Lencioni, in his book, *Five Dysfunctions* of a Team, explains this beautifully. When there is trust, there can be healthy conflict. Once people feel heard, they can commit to the decision and be held accountable for the decision they committed to. This ultimately leads to positive results.

When you face a conflict and an inability to agree on a commitment, it's worth asking, "Is this a trust issue or a technical issue?" You will be surprised to find out how many times this is a trust issue and requires an open, honest conversation with the Visionary or leadership team.

My son's principal utilizes the concept of buy-in in an amazing way. His school has a policy that, when a student misbehaves, they get called into the principal's office and have to choose their own punishment. For example, if one child bullies another child, the principal calls the boy into the office and asks him, "What do you think is the appropriate consequence when you bully another kid?" The boy says, "Missing play time," and now you know that the teacher won't have to work hard to enforce the punishment because the boy chose it himself. My son, being clever, once said he chooses no punishment. That is when the principal artfully used his communication skills and curiosity and asked him, "How am I supposed to go back to the boy you hurt and tell him that you don't want to do anything about it?" My son's immediate response was, "Fine, I will apologize to him". Little did he know this was the exact action the principal was looking for. No one gains anything from detention and timeouts.

What we are looking for when creating consequences for kids is remorse and a change of action.

The same can be said for a visionary and leadership team. When it's their idea, they have buy-in to their roles, responsibilities, Key Performance Indicators. They will be aligned with the process of how they execute the product or service because they are committed and have buy-in. Then, it is easy to hold them accountable to it because THEY chose it.

Show Them the Greater Win!

Entrepreneurs love winning, and they love a challenge. It is in their DNA. Sometimes, they will even lose money to win. They need to win even if it could be a dangerous road. A right-fit 2IC is vital to helping Visionaries gain clarity to ensure that their choices are in their best interests and for the company's greater good. Filtering is the art of clarifying when it is a shiny object that feels like a significant short-term win but can be a substantial long-term detriment is imperative. The secret sauce of success is helping Visionaries see where the real win is. Ask questions like "What do we win by not pursuing this deal right now?" or "How much more can we win if we wait?" Center your conversations around the win!

Create a Sandbox to Play In

We all know that the biggest danger to a Visionary is boredom. But what if you are such a great 2IC, you've "got this," you are holding it all together, and everything is delegated? What should the Visionary be doing?

This is where we often see chaos happening in organizations. Visionaries get bored and don't know where to channel their energy, their drive, or their gifts.

Find a challenge for the Visionary that excites them and aligns with the greater vision of the company. Assign them to explore possible mergers and acquisitions. Expand their sales network. Ask them to research technology updates.

I call this creating a sandbox for the Visionary to play in. Or you can call it organized chaos. I met a Visionary who owns a few pharmacies.

His team knows that when he comes in, he experiments with formulas, technology, and medicine. Experimentation is key for Visionaries to keep them innovative. We need them to innovate. That keeps companies and the world moving forward.

In one leadership meeting, the Visionary wanted to make a 90-day goal to make 30 sales phone calls a week. The Integrator felt compelled to make the Visionary realize that it would most probably not happen. I asked the Integrator, "Would it be so bad if this Visionary made 30 phone calls a week?". Of course, the Integrator agreed that it wouldn't be bad. "Why don't we give him that challenge?" I asked the Integrator. We gave him the challenge. The Visionary came back 90 days later and, of course, did not make the 30 weekly phone calls. We all had a great laugh. The Visionary made some good connections and also got a reality check. Now, when the team had to decide on a timeline to get into a new office building, the Visionary was a little more realistic. When he said, "Within three months, I will have a contract," we did not stop him because he needed that challenge.

Give them the BLUF (Bottom Line Up Front)

Visionaries typically prefer shorter introductions and prefaces because they typically have a short attention span. They want the meat. Get to the point. Get rid of all the fat. If you are trying to get from point A to B, the Visionary doesn't want to hear about what it will take to get from A to B. They want to hear options and possible solutions. They want to see bullet-point lists. I know this may sound curt and unemotional. Remember that most Visionaries are goal-focused, have low empathy, and are often impatient. If you need to process things more verbally, it is very important for you to find a coach or someone who can be your sounding board.

Come with Solutions, Not Problems

When speaking to Visionaries, I hear the same theme. We don't want our Integrators to bring us more problems. An Integrator's job is to find solutions.

Before you present an issue to your Visionary, think of two possible solutions to the issue and present them alongside the issue. This will show the Visionary in your life that you are proactive and future-focused. Visionaries are suspended in the future, and 2ICs tend to be trapped in the past. The goal is for both of you to become present and situation-focused.

For example: The price of your raw materials went up. Present the issue with possible alternatives of a new supplier you found or an alternative method to use. This will give the Visionary an opportunity to share his ideas, and you can jointly discover a solution.

Create Opportunities

Some Visionaries have a tendency to procrastinate concrete and necessary actions. A helpful technique is to present to-do-tasks as opportunities.

James is an integrator who fully embodies the role of running the day-to-day process for the company. When he needs the Visionary to sign-off on projects, He gives him a "window of opportunity." Hey, Mr. Visionary, we have an opportunity to extend our lease. You have until

Jan 15 to sign it. This allows James to keep the business moving forward constantly and not get stuck waiting for decisions and actions to be made. The Visionary quickly understands that opportunities have windows, and when the window closes, if you don't take the chance, sometimes it's gone forever.

Bring Them Back to the Vision.

A company vision comes from the leader. Whole companies are built around leaders—the core values, the mission, the big long-term goal, the marketing strategy, and so forth. Help your Visionary stay true to their vision by using it as a decision-making tool and constantly remind them to return to the vision. If you don't have a written vision document for your company, it is super important to sit down with your Visionary and leadership team to create one. In EOS, we call it a VTO or Vision Traction Organizer. It is a two-page document with eight simple questions that get you and your team on the same page. This ensures that you are all on the same page and see the same thing without making assumptions about what the "greater good of the company is." Decision-making is simple and easy. Remind your Visionary that your VTO is like a Pre-Made decision. You made these decisions together as a team when you were clear and level-headed and not under the immense pressure of a shiny object that fell into your lap, which is currently motivating you to stray from your Vision.

It becomes a simple question: "Does this move us closer to our vision?". Use your vision document to make decisions about the strategy used to hire and fire. Use it to determine a right-fit client. Use it at every opportunity to get a Visionary back-on-track.

Get Curious

The best way to approach any conversation is from a place of curiosity. Slow down and ask questions that will give both of you more clarity.

Simply say, "Tell me more". This creates trust and congruence in your relationship. Ask questions like "How am I supposed to do that?" to bring more rational logic into the conversation. Questions like "What do you expect from me?" can clarify expectations. I am sure you can come up with your own great questions. Keep asking "anything else" until you have a sense that you have all the information or a clear picture of what the Visionary is trying to convey.

In conclusion, in order to speak to a Visionary, you need to be your best self. You need to have great self-awareness and a healthy sense of self. Be in touch with your feelings and understand how others operate.

Do not take responsibility for other people's words, feelings, and actions as if they were your own. Instead, learn how to make them aware and guide others to take accountability for themselves.

As a 2IC, this is an essential role for you. You show the way. You are essentially the facilitator of discussions in the organization, starting with the Visionary and leadership team and cascading down to the rest of the company.

Questions to Think About:

Think of something you want the Visionary's buy-in. How can you reframe it to honor their identity of freedom and winning?

Think of a project, issue, or idea that is currently a challenge for you. What questions can you ask to get curious and help your Visionary gain clarity and buy-in?

Do you have a shared vision and long-term plan written down on paper? How do you use it to create commitment?

Which communication skill will you adapt for the coming week so that you can learn how to speak to a Visionary?

Chapter Eight
Conflict Management

Conflict is not a bad thing. It is inevitable. Healthy Visionaries and COOs, much like couples, engage in healthy conflict. In his book, *The Five Dysfunctions of a Team*, Patrick Lencioni talks about the need for healthy conflict to drive commitment, accountability, and results. As an "Other-Focused" person, you might be afraid of or tend to avoid conflict because it puts you in a position where you are seen as unkind and not nice. Often, when "Other-Focused" people avoid conflict, they just hold it all in and become a basket case. That is where communication turns from assertive to passive-aggressive. When you are holding this in because you can't handle conflict, you may slip into passive-aggressive communication.

If conflict is managed correctly, it deepens trust. It gets you even more on the same page. It is like a rope. When it is cut and then tied again, it is now shorter because the tie brought it closer.

The problem with conflict is when each side takes an opposite position and is only motivated to reinforce their position or get the other party to see their point of view. This creates gridlock. Resolution requires one side to compromise, and when that happens, neither party is happy.

Healthy conflict is about getting to the root cause and understanding the deeper motives that drives the other party. When you understand the WHY on either side of the conflict, when you understand what motivates that person and their point of view, when you understand any fears or concerns that influence their position, you can come to a totally different conclusion that is innovative and not an "either-or" resolution.

This requires using empathy, active listening, and all the tools I present in the communication section of the book. It is about getting curious and being willing to try on the other person's shoes for a minute. Ask yourself, "If I were the Visionary, how would I feel or think in this situation?" Then, the actions and commitments to resolve this conflict can be determined.

It is helpful to have boundaries and rules in conflict so both sides feel safe. Here is a list of conflict rules I collected and adapted from many marriage books because, after all, the CEO-COO relationship is the business version of a marriage.

1. Be assertive (self-valuing) rather than aggressive (getting back at the other person, no matter what the cost).

2. Stay in the now. Avoid scorekeeping and backcasting. Don't use words like "never and always." This creates an unleveled arguing field and drives you away from coming to an agreement.

3. Avoid lecturing and stay with concrete, specific details.

4. Avoid judgment and stay with self-responsible "I" messages.

5. Go for accuracy rather than agreement or perfection

6. Don't argue about details. For example, "You were 20 minutes late. No, I was only 13 minutes late".

7. Don't assign blame

8. Use active listening. Repeat what you heard them say. Get the person's agreement about what you heard before responding.

9. Argue about one thing at a time

10. Go for a solution rather than being right.

11. Get comfortable with not being a people pleaser but a vision server.

12. Get comfortable with not being liked all the time.

13. Find common ground

14. Separate truths, facts, and feelings (more about this later in the book)

15. Be honest with yourself if you are exaggerating, playing the victim, getting hysterical, or creating a situation so that you are needed (as an Other-Focused person, this might be a bad habit that is hard to break).

To be an empowered COO, it is crucial to adapt more constructive beliefs about conflicts.

Learn how to have a good fight. Get used to sitting with the discomfort of conflict. Practice hearing out the other party, even when you are mad. Intentionally embrace the fact that conflicts will inevitably happen no matter what. Change your patterns about how you deal with conflicts and you will be surprised by how much more effective and successful you will become.

Get to Know Your Differences

A practical tool that can help you understand conflicts is personality tests or profiling tools that will give you a better understanding of yourself and the visionary you work for.

There are many assessments and profiling tools that you can use to understand your unique qualities and differences. The more you know about each other and your differences, the more you learn how to live by the titanium rule: "Treat others like THEY want to be treated."

Some of my favorite profiling tools are:

Kolbe

The Kolbe system is a program that helps you understand your natural tendency on how you approach work or a task.

It helps you gain awareness of how you approach a project or decision. Do you need a lot of facts before you start a project? Are you good at following through? Do you tend to start and hope it will figure itself out?

This system will help you understand what tasks are more oriented for an Integrator vs a Visionary and how to communicate better. This assessment is all about making sure you are a perfect fit for each other. Any two profiles with greater than a 4 point difference will be a constant strain on the Visionary/Integrator relationship.

If you, as a 2IC, rate as a 2 on the quick-start scale and the Visionary is a 10 on the quick-start scale, you will always feel overwhelmed by your visionary's speed. Awareness is the first step and can help you bridge a gap.

DISC

This is an assessment that categorizes (D)ominance, (I)nfluence, (S)teadiness, and (C)onscientiousness. You can understand that if you want to successfully speak to your Visionary and manage conflicts, it is important to see how you rate on each of these aspects.

Meyers Briggs

The Myers-Briggs Type Indicator (MBTI) is a personality test that identifies four aspects of an individual's personality:

- How do you focus your attention? Are you an Extravert (E) or an Introvert (I)?

- How do you take in information? Do you use Sense (S) or do you use Intuition (I)?

- How do you make decisions? Do you Think (T) it through or go based on your Feelings (F)?

- How do you deal with the world and others? Do you Judge (J) or do you Perceive (P)?

This system generates a type based on how you score in these four aspects. Understanding how you are different or the same as your Visionary can be very helpful in communicating and managing conflicts.

Enneagram

Understanding someone's core beliefs and having insight into what motivates them can be eye opening and very helpful in the workplace. This system categorizes nine types. The Enneagram Institute offers these short descriptions. Learning more can give you the tools you need to become empowered and aware of yourself and others.

Type 1 – The Reformer

The Rational, Idealistic Type: Principled, Purposeful, Self-Controlled, and Perfectionistic

Type 2 – The Helper

The Caring, Interpersonal Type: Demonstrative, Generous, People-Pleasing, and Possessive

Type 3 – The Achiever

The Success-Oriented, Pragmatic Type: Adaptive, Excelling, Driven, and Image-Conscious

Type 4 – The Individualist

The Sensitive, Withdrawn Type: Expressive, Dramatic, Self-Absorbed, and Temperamental

Type 5 – The Investigator

The Intense, Cerebral Type: Perceptive, Innovative, Secretive, and Isolated

Type 6- The Loyalist

The Committed, Security-Oriented Type: Engaging, Responsible, Anxious, and Suspicious

Type 7 – The Enthusiast

The Busy, Fun-Loving Type: Spontaneous, Versatile, Distractible, and Scattered

Type 8 – The Challenger

The Powerful, Dominating Type: Self-Confident, Decisive, Willful, and Confrontational

Type 9 – The Peacemaker

The Easygoing, Self-Effacing Type: Receptive, Reassuring, Agreeable, and Complacent

Gallup Strength Finders (Clifton Strengths)

This assessment focuses on helping you discover your personal strengths and talents. It surveys 34 themes across four main themes of leadership.

- Executing Domain
- Influencing Domain
- Relationship Building Domain
- Strategic Thinking Domain

Getting to know each other's strengths can be key to working together and running the company effectively.

Gretchen Rubin

In your quest to become happy, healthy, and productive, it is important to find your own unique path. One way to do this is to think about the expectations you encounter. Some are outer or external, like work deadlines, and some are internal, like a personal resolution. How do you tend to respond to these expectations?

Upholders love discipline and respond to expectations well.

Questioners love to think if it makes sense and need to first be convinced in order to respond.

Obligers can easily fulfill expectations set by others but struggle to make themselves count.

Rebels resist all expectations and broadcast an attitude of 'you can't make me, and neither can I'.

If you know your tendency and the tendency of the Visionary you work with, you can set goals and conditions that will likely succeed without unnecessary stress.

Questions to Think About:

What is your biggest fear in engaging in conflict with the Visionary and leadership team?

Do you tend to shut down hard conversations?

When you engage in a heated discussion, do all parties get equal "air time"?

What can you do to get to know yourself and the Visionary better?

Chapter Nine
What Is Decisiveness?

Decisiveness is knowing and being sure of who you are at your core; your needs, triggers, hopes, dreams, strengths, and weaknesses.

How much time have you spent getting to know yourself? As someone who sits in a role that is all about helping others and realizing someone else's vision, you most probably do not spend much time discovering your own purpose and passions.

If you have not spent any time getting to know yourself, this might mean that you need to explore more to understand those needs. To understand your needs, you may need to journal and describe what you love to do, your strengths and weaknesses, where you love spending the most time, and your plan. Being decisive is about being specific about what you want and how you will get it.

Who Are You When You Aren't Serving?

A great way to discover more about your true self is to think about who you are when you aren't serving others.

Imagine you are on an island, and there is no one to take care of you. You are not a 2IC. You are not a mom or wife, a husband or father. You are just a human being.

Who are you?

What do you love to do?

What is your favorite pastime? Think about this and write it down.

Discover Your Purpose:

A key factor in helping you to become more decisive is knowing your purpose. Your WHY. Your reason for being. What fills you? This will help you discover your Empowerment Statement™. This tool is all-encompassing. Your Empowerment Statement™ is a combination of your purpose, strengths, and talent.

Why do you need a purpose? And what if my purpose is to serve others?

There are many reasons why you should have a personal purpose. But most importantly, when you know your purpose, you know what you want and why you want it. It helps you stay true to yourself so you don't lose focus and get caught in the cycle of pleasing others and abandoning yourself.

What's the difference between having a purpose of serving others versus people pleasing?

"Everyone has a purpose in life.. a unique gift or special talent to give to others. And when we blend this unique talent with service to others, we experience the ecstasy and exultation of our own spirit, which is the ultimate goal of goals."
– Deepak Chopra

Your purpose can be the guide you use when making decisions that influence your behavior, shape your goals, and create meaning in your life.

A purpose allows you to create better goals that tie to your greater purpose in life. It is a decision-making filter. When you find yourself wanting to say yes to something, ask yourself, does this fill me? Will I feel lit up? Is it my passion?

Know Your Worth:

One step is to stop and think. What is my value? What do I contribute to the world, my family, and this organization?

Develop a stronger sense of self and an Empowerment Statement[TM] by becoming aware of your strengths, weaknesses, opportunities, and threats. This is called a SWOT analysis.

Here are the four steps to building your Empowerment Statement[TM]:

Step #1 – Define your strengths

Ask three people you trust, including your Visionary, to tell you three strengths about you. What makes you great at what you do? Why do people come to you for advice? What do they believe you can do better than anyone else?

When you sit with it, you will realize a common theme from the feedback you got. What is the theme that is coming up? What do people believe about you?

One of my biggest strengths is that I have discernment as a natural ability. I am very good at filtering ideas. I also have a natural ability to bridge gaps and restore things.

I wonder what will come up for you. Another way to do this is to take the StrengthsFinder assessment from Gallup.

Step #2 – Be honest with yourself about your weaknesses

If you have what it takes, ask three people to give you constructive feedback. What are your weaknesses? What are areas that you can improve on or that are not worth your time? This is constructive feedback, so it is important not to take it personally and dwell on it.

Step #3 – Find the silver lining in your weaknesses.

Now, take it a step further and say, what is the silver lining in your weaknesses?

Ask yourself, "What's the benefit of my weakness?" Let's say my weakness is that I am not a maximizer.

I will never squeeze the bottle of toothpaste to the end. When there is still some left, I will get a new one. I think to myself, "Ugh, I am not using everything." However, when applied to other circumstances, this weakness is a good thing. In the professional world, my lack of maximization keeps people from feeling used up. I can ask for more because I will never make people feel used up.

Step #4 – Discover your passions.

What topics and activities make you lose track of time?

Make a list of the times you have been so focused you forgot about anything else.

What is my biggest accomplishment? What was your proudest moment in your current role and why?

What are people always asking you for help with?

What would you never give up for anything? When do you feel most empowered?

What do others ask you about?

What is something you do better than anyone else?

What makes you curious?

Now, it is time to incorporate your discovery into your Empowering Statement^{TM}.

I discovered that I love fixing broken things. I love restoring and bridging gaps. People see me as a great problem solver.

My Empowerment Statement^{TM} is:

"I love bridging gaps between people and issues or systems."

That is how this book and Empowered COO was born.

When you complete this tool, you will be surprised by how empowered you have become.

Go online to **www.empoweredcoo.com** to download the free Empowerment Statement[TM] worksheet that will help you discover and define your Empowerment Statement[TM].

Opportunities

Now that you know what empowers you, the question to ask is, "What opportunities are you not tapping into"?

A great way to find out is by overlaying your Empowerment Statement[TM] with your company's vision. If you are running on EOS and have a Vision Traction Organizer, take a look at your company's mission statement and ask yourself, "Where do I come into the picture? Where do my strengths come into play? Where am I the most needed?" That is how you can be your best self, showing up every day in your role while letting go and delegating the things that don't fit your

Empowerment Statement[TM] because it is not the best use of your time. As the glue that holds the organization together, your time is extremely valuable.

Now, think, where else in your life are you not tapping into opportunities? What passions are you not exploring?

What have you always dreamed of doing, but fear has kept you from doing it? Is it something you have fantasized about for a long time?

Volunteer, hike the Appalachian trail, go back to school, become a flight attendant or a public speaker. Why haven't you started working towards it? Is it because you are afraid to try something new or fear you'll fail?

Create a list of opportunities that if you had no fear, if nothing held you back, what would you spend your time doing?

Threats

Do you know what the biggest threat standing in the way of you being your highest self, the person who feels fulfilled, confident, and empowered and executing flawlessly as a 2IC that drives execution?

Your biggest threat is neglecting to take care of yourself. Believing that you must put others first, that it's okay, that you don't have needs, or that you will take care of yourself another time (which usually never happens).

It is important to become better at creating self-care and a vision for yourself from a big-picture perspective to the everyday little details and routines like sitting for two minutes in silence with your coffee.

You cannot pour from an empty cup. When your cup is full, you can give to others. As someone who is in a supportive role, you are constantly giving and being there for others. Your only way of survival and the best way to thrive is by living by the "put on your oxygen mask first" rule.

You might have to start by gaining basic knowledge about yourself. What do you love to do? What type of vacations do you like? For many years, my go-to vacations were beach resorts. It's where my friends and family have always wanted to go, so I just said yes. Once, I ended up in Arizona, staring at beautiful mountains, I discovered that I love mountains. I finally admitted to myself that I have a fear of water and beaches make me anxious. Now, I have a yearly goal of taking one mountain vacation a year. I find serenity in the mountains, but in the past, I never gave myself the luxury of discovering my preferences. I never asked myself, "What is my favorite activity outside of work? How do I love to spend time? What is my favorite color? What are my favorite foods?"

Create a personal vision plan that includes your Empowerment Statement^{TM}, bucket list, long-term vision, and daily routine to elucidate your self-care, needs, passions, and aspirations at your deepest level.

Check out **www.empoweredcoo.com** for free resources and download a free Daily Empowerment Self-Care Checklist.

If you feel guilty about taking time to get to know yourself and care for yourself, I want to tell you about your next biggest threat to being the Empowered COO you are meant to be.

Resentment

What happens when you fail to care for yourself?

When you watch the Visionary taking time off by randomly calling in and saying, "Sorry, I will not make it today," while you never ask for time off because you are afraid to ask or think you don't deserve it. When the Visionary takes vacations, and you haven't taken a vacation in three years. The Visionary is living the life of their dreams because you, the COO, dedicates your lifetime of work to the Visionary's organization.

A little seed of resentment starts to grow. You try to wish it away, excuse it, but it just swells and grows till you cannot ignore it anymore. It hovers over you like a shadow. At meetings, at events, when you are at work, and when you go home. Unless you address the resentment you are feeling, you will turn into a basket case that will eventually implode.

What resentments may indicate is neglect in your self-care needs. Many 2ICs find themselves secretly resentful, and they do not know how to handle it. That is a big part of the challenges we discuss at the beginning of the book.

My coach, Kelly Clemens, taught me that resentment and anger are an invitation to ask yourself, "What am I seeing in the other person that I am not getting, want, or may also need?" Resentment and anger are jealousy. But no one likes to admit to being jealous, so we cover it up as anger and festering anger is resentment.

When you find resentment creeping up, take it as an invitation to ask yourself, "What am I missing that I want or need and can give myself to fill myself up?"

On a personal level, in a marriage, a lot of times, one partner has the narrative that, "Oh, my husband/wife gets to go out and party or have a night out, and I cannot do that. I have to take care of the kids." The question is, who said you can't go out and have a good time, too? Maybe you need to arrange childcare. Maybe your version of doing something for yourself is taking a bath or going for a walk.

Having a list of self-care things that you can give yourself makes it easy to ask yourself this question in the midst of the storm and give yourself an actionable task that can ground you without having to exhaust yourself with the decision-making process.

This leads me to the next threat of being an Empowered COO.

Boundaries

Boundaries are about knowing where you begin and where you end. Where do your responsibilities and identity begin and end?

Codependence, at its core, is a lack of or weak boundaries. It is over-committing yourself and saying yes when you really want to say no. It is about letting people invade your personal space and letting people drain you emotionally or take up too much of your time and energy, which later leads to resentment.

Giving someone more than you wanted or agreed to give is a perfect recipe for resentment.

Many 2ICs have poor time management skills because they lack boundaries around allocating and committing time. You spend too much time being a therapist to draining team members and don't know how to be assertive and end meetings or vent sessions. This can cause you to be late for your next meeting or leave you no time for yourself to fulfill your roles and responsibilities.

This goes back to the need to feel needed and the fear of not being liked. If you will enforce your boundary and be assertive, what will the other person think? How will they see you? Therefore, you choose to betray yourself and your commitments just to please and look good to the other person (albeit temporarily because often a lack of boundaries backfires).

Oversharing personal information also comes from a lack of boundaries. Do you ever find yourself sharing information and later regretting it? Who do you owe explanations for the decisions you made? As a 2IC, you make the call on day-to-day decisions, and when you doubt yourself and give too much information, it opens you up to constant negotiation and pushback.

People are often confused about what boundaries are. They think boundaries should be announced and imposed on the people around you and aggressively enforced. This can set you up for failure because Visionaries find challenges thrilling. Imposing a boundary on a Visionary is essentially giving them an opportunity for a thrilling challenge. By nature, Visionaries are rule-breakers. That is what makes them amazing and that is what makes them innovators. Thomas Edison invented the light bulb by challenging the status quo.

Boundaries are not for them. They are for you. Boundaries are internal. They are a commitment to yourself. They are a way to take control of your inventory – your finite resources, your time, energy, intellect, and material and physical possessions.

How much time do you want to give to listen to somebody? You will notice that giving somebody too much time makes you feel exhausted, burnt-out, and resentful. How much time do you want to spend at networking events? Do you know the boundary of when it is too much for you? I know that if I go out more than once a week, I am exhausted the second time and cannot be the person I want to be if I go over my boundaries.

You must decide what your boundaries are, what your commitment to yourself is, and how YOU will keep that commitment.

Clarifying Boundaries and Inner Circle

Setting boundaries starts with clarifying who your trusted people are. Who are the people in your life and work environment that deserve your time, energy, and resources?

How do you qualify them?

Who is in your middle and outer circle?

What information do you share with inner circle people but not middle or outer?

There are five types of boundaries in the workplace.

Physical Boundaries

This is your personal space and physical touch. This includes your office, desk, emails. Your physical boundaries are violated when others don't consider your personal space.

Intellectual Boundaries

This is your thoughts and ideas. It also involves respect and awareness of others' ideas and what is appropriate to discuss with whom.

Your intellectual boundaries are crossed when a person criticizes or dismisses your ideas or is intrusive and picks your brain beyond your comfort level.

Emotional Boundaries

This refers to your feelings. Having healthy emotional boundaries is knowing when to share, when not to share, who to share with, and how others treat you emotionally.

Your emotional boundaries are violated when someone belittles you, criticizes you, or makes you feel that your feelings are unimportant.

Material Boundaries

This refers to money and possessions; who to share your possessions with and getting paid appropriately.

Material boundaries are violated when someone takes or damages your possessions or when you are pressured by someone to give your possessions to them.

Time Boundaries

This refers to the use of your time, how you choose to spend your time, and with whom and having enough time for the people who are most important to you, starting with yourself. Your time boundaries are violated when another person demands too much of your time.

How do you decide when it's time to set a boundary?

Here are some questions to ask yourself:

Am I angry?

Am I resentful?

Do I feel used?

Do I feel violated?

Do I feel isolated?

Do I feel frightened?

Do I feel treated less than?

Are my boundaries allowing me to do my best work and show up as my best self?

For each of these boundaries, decide who in your life gets to have how much of your energy, intellect, time, material, and emotion.

Decide how you will re-enforce the boundary if it is broken. Remember to use the communication tools from the previous chapter.

Re-enforcing boundaries should keep the focus on you, not on the other person. For example, instead of "Stop asking me personal questions," the re-enforcement of your privacy boundary is "I am not ready to talk about this yet – it is too personal."

When you find yourself failing to keep a boundary, ask yourself, "What deep-rooted belief causes me to betray myself?"

"What do I fear?"

Not being liked? Being rejected? Being called selfish?

You also need to decide the natural consequences that will follow. This is where your empowerment comes in and will be the deciding factor in creating permanent change.

Maybe your natural consequence is that if a team member continues to talk down to you, then you will only communicate by email. Maybe if the Visionary takes up too much of your time, you will be curt and walk away. You must be ready to enforce your consequences, so choose wisely and find support. Choose logical, predictable, and consistent consequences. Do not create room for arguments. Support yourself in reminding yourself that you deserve respect, honor, and consideration as a basic human right.

Download the free Boundary Worksheet at **www.empoweredcoo.com/freeworkbook** to discover and create your boundaries.

What Is on Your List?

You and your Visionary should both have two lists to help you get abundantly clear of what your expectations are of each other.

I do this with all COOs that I work with.

Create a **"Wish List"** and a **"Non-Negotiable List."**

A wish list is all the hopes, ideas, and dreams that the Visionary wants you to accomplish. Overhauling systems, implementing tools, innovating processes, etc.

On your wish list are things you want from your Visionary. Is it an end-of-year bonus? A perk? Anything that you expect or want?

The non-negotiable list is things that are deal breakers for you.

One Visionary has a non-negotiable that emails must be responded to within 24 hours. It is important to him and the culture he wants in the business. The customer service and the speed. When the 2IC understands how important it is to the Visionary, she is able to enforce it and execute it organization-wide.

On the 2ICs non-negotiable list, there should be things that are deal breakers for you. Time off? A behavior you expect? Leaving work every day at a certain time?

Once you learn how to identify your needs and boundaries better, you can create a non-negotiable list which will be a safety net and provide you with the knowledge that your needs and wants will be attended to.

What Are Your Non-Negotiables?

When I was an assistant during a personal vision workshop for Integrators at the FIM or Female Integrator Mastermind Summit, I spoke to a few women who mentioned their "term" or "contract" was up, and they were considering what to do next. Retire? Become a Fractional

Integrator? Start a business? One woman said she's buying a stable and horses and is going to devote her time to farming. These women were stronger, better Integrators because they didn't feel like there was no life past their current role.

Perhaps it is time for 2ICs to go on a contract basis since the average engagement of a COO is 2.5-5 years.

Like that, a few things will happen that will empower YOU, the Second-in-Command.

You will set the terms and conditions of the engagement; this enables you to negotiate and ask for what you want and to be assertive.

Another important factor is your need for security. You have a right to plan for your future and create a sense of security for yourself. As a Second-In-Command, it is fair to say that you put your life and soul into a business that most probably isn't yours. You work hard, minus the risk that a Visionary carries. At the end of the day, when payroll isn't covered, it is the Visionary who doesn't sleep at night. But that doesn't mean that you shouldn't be compensated appropriately. Whether that means a buy-in option or bonuses based on performance and growth, if you are compensated appropriately, you will feel less burnt out.

A personal long-term plan is important because you want to design your life before someone designs it for you. If you have no goals and aspirations, then you just swim with the tide and end up somewhere in a few years from now, looking back and saying, "How did I get here?"

Alex Freytag just released his second book on the subject of employee compensation titled "Stretch Not Snap" Create a Self-Funded Incentive Plan, End Employee Entitlement, and Get Your Vision Shared by All. I recommend reading it along with his book "Profit Works" on how to create incentive plans that reward performance.

All of the above-mentioned factors impact your ability to be decisive. Discovering who you are, creating your Empowerment Statement[TM,] learning to set boundaries, and making sure you are adequately compensated will help you be more decisive.

Questions to Think About:

What is your greatest strength as a Second-In-Command?

How can you make your weakness a strength?

What opportunities are you not stepping into?

What boundaries do you struggle with most?

What is your fear in setting boundaries?

What are specific actions you can take to set boundaries?

Chapter Ten
What Is Discernment?

Discernment is to judge well. It is the power to discern good from bad, to home in on your sense of intuition. When you have good discernment skills, you prosper even when times are tough. Discernment is essential when a crisis hits, something happens, or a decision needs to be made. People who struggle with discernment make costly mistakes and fail to succeed.

Discernment does not have a formula. You can't take a class on discernment, yet it is the most essential skill of successful COOs.

Discernment comes with experience and self-awareness. It comes with knowing your preferences and boundaries.

Discernment encompasses everything you do as the Second-in-Command. It involves taking the Visionary ideas, filtering the good from the bad, and creating a plan of action.

Being good at discerning takes practice and involves trial and error. It takes constantly referencing your preferences and boundaries and what is tried and proven.

It is making decisions based on data rather than emotion. I always say never make the same mistake twice. I will make one mistake once, but I will never make the same mistake twice. I have a Rolodex in my brain of mistakes I made, and I change course when I see something familiar coming.

When I started writing this book, I almost repeated a mistake. Somehow, I found myself sitting in a conference room with somebody who was taking over my project, like this book; they wanted to change the title and content. I went home and thought, "Wait, this feels very familiar. It feels like I have been there." That means I have already experienced this and made this mistake.

This was being in touch with my intuition, trusting and listening to my gut about how I felt in that meeting, and making the right decision.

Here are areas where discernment is essential and needs to be exercised:

Separating Truth, Facts, Feelings

To be an effective decision maker, who is the tie-breaker and makes the day-to-day decisions of the company, it is crucial for you to keep an objective view and separate truth, facts and not get sucked into feelings.

Because of the Other-Focused nature of a 2IC, you run the risk of blurring facts with feelings. You tend to confuse feelings with facts, which makes an issue look bigger and scarier and often impossible to solve, leading you to negative self-talk like "this will never work out", "this is too big to solve", or "this is colossal". For the situation to be resolved, you need to focus on constructive actions. Emotional and dramatic responses paralyze the organization and ruin relationships.

Through coaching many COOs, I have found that a COO is often afraid to make a tough decision or have a challenging conversation because of their own personal narrative and feelings about rejection or outcomes.

When I work with COOs to help them separate truth, facts, and feelings, I find that the top feelings that hold back COOs are fear of rejection and feeling incompetent.

Here is what it can look like: You are reviewing P&L reports and are realizing the business is not making as much money as the visionary thinks it is. You are afraid to have this conversation with the visionary. Why are you afraid? Are you afraid that the visionary will reject the claims and instead say you aren't doing a good job? That you are not trying hard enough? Maybe if you make them aware of the financial status they might make the decision to let go of you. Although you are valuable to the company, you might also be in the highest paid position.

Another example: You feel that a team member isn't the right fit to be on the leadership team, and their role must be changed. You are afraid to have this conversation with the visionary and instead keep procrastinating while this issue festers and takes up a lot of your time.

In each of these situations, it is important to separate the Truths, Facts, and Feelings before approaching a conversation and making a decision.

Ask yourself, what am I afraid of? How do I feel about this person or decision? Is there a personal agenda here? Be honest with yourself. Once you do that, take time to work through those feelings. Am I as incompetent as those naughty voices in my head say I am? If I delay this issue, how will it affect me later? Why am I afraid to be rejected? Do I not know my value?

Once you get the feelings out of the way, you can tackle the data. Do you have data to back up your claims and decisions? Can you prove that this person is not performing? Do you have reports that you can show projections and outcomes of the investment you are opposing?

Now, you can move on to the truth. Remember that there is no one truth. The ultimate truth is God's truth. Remember that you are seeing life through the filter of your experiences. What is true today might not be true tomorrow. What is your truth, might not be the Visionary's truth.

The Pandemic is a great example of how truths change. In March 2020, everyone assumed masks would prevent people from getting covid. However, the facts about what happened in 2020 remain the same. The truth may have changed.

Pleasing vs Serving

Another area of discernment is being able to differentiate when you are pleasing people over serving them and the greater good of the organization. Because 2ICs tend to be people-pleasers, we sometimes lose the vision of the bigger picture and get caught in the minutiae, the details, and the person. We might put the Visionary on a pedestal and end up pleasing them versus the vision they want, which they elucidated clearly in a lucid moment. It is important that when a Visionary makes a request, you ask yourself, "Am I pleasing the Visionary, or am I serving the greater good of the organization?"

Practice a Word Diet

Other focused 2ICs tend to want to anticipate other people's needs (especially the Visionary's) because it makes you look useful. Yet, this can be detrimental because it puts you in the position of becoming a mind reader, and people will overly rely on you. People react the way we act towards them, and if we train them to rely on us to anticipate their needs, they will rely on us to constantly pick up their slack. This includes solving people's problems for them instead of teaching your leadership team to become problem solvers. It's teaching a person to fish versus feeding them.

In my coaching practice, I recommend COOs that I work with practice a word diet. This means using a ratio of 80/20. The largest chunk of time, 80% should be dedicated to asking questions. The immediate result is that only 20% of the time must be focused on providing solutions. If you practice getting curious and asking questions instead of leading the visionary and providing direct reports, the questions themselves provide the best answer. This is a fun challenge, and for some of my clients, it translates to the rest of the leadership team. The more members who adapt the word diet and keep focused on asking questions, the more effective the organization will become. This is discernment in real-life practice.

Discerning Root Causes

As a 2IC and COO, you are accountable for facilitating healthy discussions and determining a plan of action. The only way to do that effectively is to determine the root cause of the issue. An empowered COO is notorious for digging down to the root cause of an issue and not bandaging symptoms. This might be uncomfortable and hard to do at first because it requires pushing your team to have hard, uncomfortable conversations. But, like anything else, it is like exercising a muscle. After your first workout, you feel sore all over. After the first few hard conversations, it feels very uncomfortable. After your tenth workout, your body no longer feels sore, and after adapting a pattern of having difficult conversations, everyone on the team will attain a comfort level to communicate directly.

Good and Bad Advice

It is easy to get carried away by people's ideas and opinions, especially when they are from trusted people and sources. It is important to determine what qualifies this person to give this advice. What is this person's interest, and what are the consequences? Fact check advice. It is called "Trust but Verify".

Investment vs. Gamble

Visionaries, being thrill seekers and risk takers, rely on you, the Second-in-Command's intuition to steer clear of bad investments. This is because you are hardwired differently than a Visionary and are more logical. Knowing that this is your gift is a strength in itself. Using cost and benefit analysis and not making blind assumptions will assure that you aren't taking gambles but making wise investments.

It is easy for a 2IC to constantly want to stay the course and not re-route. But sometimes, the situation requires a change of course. Using your skills of discernment, using facts and data, will help you be more comfortable when change is needed.

Delegating

A big part of being a center-focused 2IC is knowing what should be on your plate and what should not. It is about not taking on other people's issues and monkeys, setting boundaries, and knowing what is yours to tackle and what is for others. Using the tools I shared previously to discover your strengths and the Empowerment Statement™ will help you determine the best use of your time and energy.

Look at your list of tasks and ask yourself, "Is this my strength? Can I do this? Is this the best use of my time?" If it is not, find the right person to give this over to. A great 2IC doesn't do the work for the team. An empowered COO shows and guides the team on how to do their best work.

Predicting and Prioritizing

Predicting and prioritizing is another skill that comes with discernment. This is essential. Do you know what is most important? Are you clear about what the highest priority is for the success of the team and company? I often find 2ICs spending too much time on the details that don't matter because they get paralyzed and have not strengthened their skill of prioritization.

People will constantly be vying for your time and attention. Determine what is urgent, most important, short-term, and long-term, and prioritize who and what is most important or can wait. This is essential in your role.

Control the Controllables

When it comes to being a problem solver, it is easy to get carried away in the "what if?". Are you thinking about things that are out of your control? When you find yourself in a situation that feels out of control, remind yourself to focus on controlling the controllables. The stock market is plummeting. What can you control? Your investments, your plan B, your attitude. Many times, as a 2IC, we believe we need to have everything under control, but the truth is that you will find yourself in plenty of situations where things happen that are out of your control. A Visionary can make an unexpected pivot, markets change, or a team is expanded. Remember, your attitude and reactions are always in your control.

Who Are You?

The greatest discernment you can do is discerning who you are as a leader.

What is your leadership style? What do you stand for?

There is this saying, "You have got to fake it till you make it." Becoming the person you want to be takes a lot of faking until you become that person. In the book, "How to Be a Great Boss", Gino Wickman, talks about leadership, management, and accountability. On the first page, it says, "As a leader, come as who you are. You don't need to change. But most importantly, you need to care about people and want to be at your best." But who are you? That is the question to ask. Come as you may, yes, but who are you??

You want to develop a leader avatar, like a person you can pretend to be externally. It is a mask that you can put on that you can grow into, that is assertive, decisive, and discerning, and that you will become. Do you want to be the sweet grandma, or do you want to be the drill sergeant? Become clear about what leader you are so you can step into your truest, most empowered self.

Questions to Think About:

Do you trust your sense of intuition?

What is one thing you can identify right now that you can delegate?

What is one thing that is tedious and unimportant that you have been spending too much time on?

If no one would judge you, what type of leader would you want to be seen as?

Chapter Eleven
Who is Your Puppeteer?

So, we have finally arrived at the closing remarks. I want to leave you with this thought.

By now, you have learned so much about the difference between Visionaries and anyone who takes their supportive role. You understand your differences on a genetic level. It is abundantly clear that Visionaries have a love and need to win. They also set the bar high. Unrealistically high. Great CEOs like Elon Musk and Steve Jobs are notoriously known for setting unrealistic expectations and goals. They will shorten deadlines and cut budgets because it gives them that thrill. When they do succeed in making those impossible goals happen, they feel like the victorious hero. "I made the impossible possible," the ultimate adrenaline rush!

Every Visionary's response to this accusation will be, "Well, if I wouldn't set an impossible goal or deadline, we wouldn't even have gotten to the original goal."

But when a Visionary fails, they are mad and sad for a minute, maybe a day. When the first three rocket launches failed, Elon Musk may have spent 15 minutes, or perhaps a few hours tops, to get over it. He must have very quickly charged onto the next project. In fact, once, as the rocket was exploding mid-air, he announced on the loudspeaker that this was a success because failing fast lets you improve and move forward faster. Driven Visionaries get up and dust off and try again and again and again. They are hardwired for this.

On the other hand, when they win, they barely take a minute to acknowledge and celebrate. They have something Dr. Doug Brackmann calls "Success Amnesia" it is in their DNA. They right away fantasize about the bigger and better. When you deliver a 3-tiered cake, they say, "Imagine if this had 4 tiers, how much more mega would it be?" It's not because they don't like the 3-tiered cake, it's because they are already onto the next but forgot to acknowledge the present, what's right in front of them, and to acknowledge all the people and hard work it took to make a 3-tiered cake. They tend to live in the "Gap," not in the "Gain," a term and book popularized by Dan Sullivan, founder of Strategic Coach.

The bottom line is that they always want MORE.

It's not all bad. It's amazing, actually. They keep the world going around, constantly producing bigger and better. It's how we got AI, social media, and driverless cars.

But it is a buy one, get one free deal.

Your success lies in acknowledging, accepting, and appreciating this.

In contrast, in a supportive role, your barometer of success is others' validation of you. As one 2IC related to me, "I set my barometer of success on what I perceive is others acknowledging of what success is." How does a 2IC know if they did a good job? Well, if they bring the Visionary's ideas into reality, create freedom for the Visionary, and show them appreciation and acknowledgment, then they know they did a good job.

So basically, your success is dependent on the Visionary's expectations of you, while the

A Visionary's success is dependent on their expectations of themselves (which they are super flexible and forgiving of, by the way), and you tend to be hard on yourself.

But what if those Visionaries are constantly moving the goalposts? And enough is never enough? In truth, there is no end goal to life and business goals. We want to constantly keep growing. If we stay still, we die. Jim Collins has proven that in his book "Good to Great" businesses that reach their long-term goals were the beginning of their demise.

So how can you, as a Second-in-Command, feel successful, accomplished, and worthwhile on this roller coaster journey?

The answer is in the tools that I presented to you in this book. Know your worth, understand your mission and passion – what fills you, have a personal vision, and set boundaries. Build your self-confidence and have a healthy dose of Self-Focus. Take ownership of your feelings and reactions. Say what you mean; mean what you say.

When you have all this, you don't let others be your puppeteers. You don't let others decide for you if you are successful and accomplishing. You know it deep inside yourself. No one needs to tell you (although it is always nice to hear it, of course). This will make you into an assertive, respected leader. You will step into your power as a COO and be the hero of the Visionary and the advocate of your leadership team!

Here's How We Can Help You

From Theory to Integration: Your Superpower

You were chosen for this critical leadership role because of your talents and potential to turn visions into reality. But the path from being the "best person in the room" to a confident 2IC who unleashes growth is steep. Without the right tools, you may feel overwhelmed navigating the gap between big dreams and everyday execution.

This book charts your journey to finding your voice, establishing boundaries, and leading effectively alongside your Visionary.

You will discover your unique abilities and learn to create an empowering "leadership avatar," communicate in a way that is heard, and have the ability to discern confidently. Become the respected, Empowered COO your company needs.

To learn more about the ideas discussed in this book, go to **www.empoweredcoo.com**

Step 1: Take the Empowered COO assessment at **www.empoweredcoo.com/assessment**

Step 2: Download the Boundary worksheet to help you empower yourself.

www.empoweredcoo.com/freeworkbook

Step 3: Get in touch about personal coaching and online courses to practice all the skills outlined in the book and to empower yourself.

Made in United States
Troutdale, OR
11/24/2024